RJ

The Effectiveness of
Antitrust Policy towards
Horizontal Mergers

Research in Business Economics and Public Policy, No. 1

Fred Bateman, Series Editor

Chairman and Professor
Business Economics & Public Policy
Indiana University

Other Titles in This Series

The Effectiveness of Antitrust Policy towards Horizontal Mergers

by
David B. Audretsch

UMI RESEARCH PRESS
Ann Arbor, Michigan

Produced and distributed by
UMI Research Press
an imprint of
University Microfilms International
Ann Arbor, Michigan 48106

Library of Congress Cataloging in Publication Data

Audretsch, David B.
The effectiveness of antitrust policy towards
horizontal mergers.

(Research in business economics and public policy ;
no. 1)
Revision of the author's thesis—University of Wisconsin-
Madison, 1980.
Bibliography: p.
Includes index.
1. Trusts, Industrial—United States. 2. Consolidation and
merger of corporations—United States. 3. Industry and state
—United States. 1. Title. II. Title: Antitrust policy toward
horizontal mergers. III. Series.

HD2795.A84 1983   338.8'042   83-6985
ISBN 0-8357-1434-9

To my parents, Helen and Leo Audretsch

Contents

List of Figures

List of Tables

Acknowledgments

This study is the culmination of three years as a student under Leonard W. Weiss at the University of Wisconsin. During this time he continually stressed and showed through his example the value of asking important questions and answering them adhering to the highest standards of intellectual integrity. He applied the same patience and encouragement in supporting this research as he did in teaching the graduate seminar in industrial organization. I am grateful to Professor Weiss for all his assistance.

Professor Willard F. Mueller provided several key suggestions both in the development of this study and in its final version. By sharing his experiences and knowledge of antitrust and economics with me he has helped to enrich this study.

1

Introduction

Overview

In 1950 President Harry S. Truman signed the Celler-Kefauver Act into law. This statute did much more than eliminate a loophole based on a legal technicality; it symbolized renewed Congressional concern and vigorous commitment to the preservation of competitive markets and the prevention of monopoly power. One commentator was moved to write, "Thus, over 40 years after the enactment of the Clayton Act, it now becomes apparent for the first time that Section 7 has been a giant all along."[1]

Yet satisfaction with the new antimerger law has not been universal among economists. John Kenneth Galbraith argues that because the Act ". . . exempts those who possess the market power and concentrates on those who would try to possess it" its enforcement ". . . defends and gives legitimacy to a charade."[2]

Is enforcement of the Celler-Kefauver Act, along with the broader purpose of antitrust policy, a "charade," an anachronism in a complex industrial society? This study investigates one aspect of the antitrust laws—horizontal merger enforcement of the Clayton Act—and attempts to answer that question. By comparing the benefits with the costs of undertaking horizontal merger cases, an evaluation of Celler-Kefauver enforcement is possible.

This introductory chapter provides a historical perspective on the antitrust laws in general, with particular emphasis on the Celler-Kefauver Act. Such a perspective is essential in a study examining the effectiveness of horizontal merger enforcement, since the social benefits from antitrust are rooted in legislative history. Therefore, based on earlier research, the Congressional intent behind the antitrust laws will be identified, along with the development of the Celler-Kefauver Act.

The Goals of Antitrust

What are the basic goals underlying antitrust policy? What did Congress have in mind when enacting the various antitrust statutes? These questions are as important as they are difficult to answer; without a clear conception of the purpose of the antitrust laws it is impossible to identify the social benefits from their enforcement. Despite this importance, the goals of antitrust remain elusive. F. M. Scherer, who was Director of the Bureau of Economics at the Federal Trade Commission from 1974 to 1976, found Congressional intent "muddled and often contradictory." He observed, "I frequently felt that if we only knew precisely where we're to go, we could proceed there in a more orderly fashion. But clear objectives were a luxury we seldom enjoyed, ambiguity was our guiding star."[3]

Despite, or because of, this confusion, considerable attention has been devoted to identifying the Congressional purpose behind the antitrust laws. One researcher has warned that the construct of legislative intent must be used carefully, ". . . if for no other reason than its inherent artificiality."[4] Robert Bork, for example, is convinced that allocative efficiency was not only the dominant, but the sole consideration of Congress in enacting the antitrust statutes. After reviewing the legislative history prior to the Sherman Act, he reports, "My conclusion, drawn from the evidence in the Congressional Record is that Congress intended the courts to implement only that value we would today call consumer welfare. To put it another way, the policy the courts were intended to apply is the maximization of wealth or consumer want satisfaction."[5]

Bork leaves no room for possible ambiguity about his interpretation: "Though an economist of our day would describe the problem of concern to (Senator) Sherman differently, as a misallocation of resources brought about by a restriction of output rather than one of the high prices, there is no doubt that Sherman and he would be thinking the same thing."[6]

Not all economists agree about the single-mindedness of Congress in passing the antitrust laws. Leonard W. Weiss interprets the primary intent of Congress as concern over the redistribution of wealth as a result of monopoly power: "It seems doubtful whether Congress gave much, if any weight to allocative efficiency when formulating the antitrust laws, while the prevention of large capital gains to those who organized monopolistic cartels or mergers is probably a major concern of the public in its commitment to competition."[7] Weiss, perhaps acknowledging the fact that the concept of allocative efficiency was barely at the frontier of economic theory while Senator Sherman and his colleagues were engaged in debate, concludes that ". . . it seems certain that Congress never thought in terms of the welfare triangle when it passed the antitrust laws and that the public and Congress do not concern themselves with it today."[8]

Willard F. Mueller attributes broader, non-economic as well as economic goals to Congressional motivation underlying the Celler-Kefauver Act: ". . . while Congress spoke much about broad economic, social, and political consequences of economic power, when it wrote a statute to cope with these problems it applied an economic concept, the probable lessening of competition within particular geographic and product markets. It is important to keep in mind this distinction between the objectives of the act and the statutory language."[9]

Certainly Mueller's interpretation of Congressional intent is consistent with Senator Sherman, who argued for passage of his 1890 bill because, "If we will not endure a King as a political power we should not endure a King over the production, transportation, and sale of the necessaries of life. If we would not submit to an emperor we should not submit to an autocrat of trade with power to prevent competition and to fix the price of any commodity."[10]

The goal of antitrust policy is apparently multidimensional. It includes the prevention and elimination of monopoly prices and restricted output, the redistribution of wealth away from monopolists, and the diffusion and decentralization of aggregate concentration of economic resources in society. This study operationalizes the goals of antitrust as two widely respected economic and social values: (1) the redistribution of wealth, and (2) allocative efficiency. However, it should be remembered that the gain to society from antitrust enforcement may include more than these two types of benefits.

The Development of the Celler-Kefauver Act

The earliest antimerger policy began with the Sherman Act, which was passed in 1890. This law contained general language prohibiting combinations in restraint of trade in the form of trusts. In two early cases reaching the Supreme Court, *Northern Securities Co. v. U.S.*[11] and *Standard Oil v. U.S.*,[12] it was established that unless an acquisition created or enhanced a monopoly, mergers were beyond the reach of the Sherman Act. The great merger wave at the turn of the century[13] provided glaring evidence of the inability of the Sherman Act to control merger activity. In fact, based on historical merger patterns, George J. Stigler concluded, "The Sherman Law seems to have been the fundamental cause for the shifts from merger for monopoly to merger for oligopoly. Sometimes its workings were obvious, as when Standard Oil was dismembered and when the leading banking mergers were prevented from combining. More often, its workings have been more subtle: the ghost of Senator Sherman is an ex officio member of the board of directors of every large company."[14]

Thus, in 1914, responding to sentiment to arrest further industrial consolidation, Congress passed the Clayton Act. From the Congressional debates it is apparent that both the House and Senate intended a statute that would deter monopoly in its incipiency. David D. Martin reports, "The ideas expressed . . . from the debates all show a desire to implement the policy of the Sherman Act by prohibiting some trade practices because they lead to the development of monopoly, rather than because they lessen competition and increase monopoly power."[15]

Acting on this conviction, Congress decreed in Section 7

> That no corporation engaged in commerce shall acquire, directly or indirectly, the whole or any part of the stock or other share capital of another corporation engaged also in commerce where the effect of such acquisition may be to substantially lessen competition between the corporation whose stock is so acquired and the corporation making the acquisition, or to restrain such commerce in any section or community or tend to create a monopoly of any line of commerce.[16]

Despite the intention of Congress, the original Section 7 of the Clayton Act was ineffective for three major reasons. The first and most publicized deficiency was that the Act applied only to stock acquisitions. Thus, the law could be easily circumvented by acquiring a firm's assets instead of its stock. The seriousness of this omission in the statute became obvious in a series of cases heard by the Supreme Court in the 1920s, culminating in the *Arrow-Hart and Hegeman Electric Company v. FTC*[17] case in 1934: "In 1934 in a five to four decision, the Supreme Court dealt the apparent death blow to Section 7 of the Clayton Act by holding that even though a complaint was issued prior to the acquisition of properties, the Commission could not order the divestment of the properties."[18]

The second deficiency in enforcement of the original Clayton Act was that the judicial interpretation seemed to imply that only horizontal mergers were covered by the law. According to Martin, "The Supreme Court's interpretation of the standard of illegality did place undue restrictions on the Federal Trade Commission. In the first place, it required that the Commission find evidence that the acquiring and the acquired companies had been in competition with each other in the sense that they were each selling the same product or products in the same markets. A substantial proportion of the sales of each firm were required to be of the common product. . . ."[19]

The third major impediment to effective Clayton 7 enforcement was the standard of proof required by the court to obtain a conviction: ". . . the court required that the probable effect of the acquisition must be to injure the public by substantially lessening competition in the industry. The most important restriction was that the court required that proof be essentially the same as the proof required for a Sherman Act violation."[20]

The enforcement record of the antitrust agencies under the original Section 7 reflected these deficiencies. Between 1914 and 1950 the Department of Justice and the FTC challenged seventy-nine mergers, but sixteen were essentially Sherman Section 2 cases. Of the fifty-eight complaints filed by the FTC, forty-eight were dismissed, and eleven obtained cease and desist orders requiring divestiture. However, eight of these were appealed and in six cases the order was substantially modified, resulting in five dissolutions and one modified divestiture. The enforcement record was somewhat more sucessful at the Justice Department. Ten out of twenty Section 7 cases achieved some form of stock divestiture, although often in a modified version.[21]

As a result of this emasculation, the original antimerger statute was amended by the Celler-Kefauver Act in 1950 to close the loopholes. Congressman Estes Kefauver explained the purpose of the Amendment, "The bill is not complicated. It proposes simply to plug the loophole in sections 7 and 11 of the Clayton Act."[22] Hence, the Celler-Kefauver Amendment to the Clayton Act was passed, altering the first paragraph of Section 7 to

> That no corporation engaged in commerce shall acquire directly or indirectly, the whole or any part of the stock or other share capital, and no corporation subject to the jurisdiction of the Federal Trade Commission shall acquire the whole or any part of the assets of another corporation engaged also in commerce where in any line of commerce in any section of the country the effect of such acquisition may be substantially to lessen competition or tend to create a monopoly.[23]

By changing the wording of the original Section 7, the Celler-Kefauver Act included asset acquisitions into its jurisdiction and modified the standard of illegality. The antitrust agencies no longer had to bear the same burden of proof required by Sherman Act standards. The emphasis on the concepts of "substantial lessening of competition" and "tendency to create monopoly" demonstrated Congressional concern at preventing mergers that *might* lead to monopoly power.

Evaluating Horizontal Merger Enforcement

The 1950 Amendment did not escape the attention of economists. Throughout the 1950s, 1960s, and 1970s, particular concern was devoted to the impact of the "new" Clayton Act on merger patterns and economic concentration. Jesse Markham articulates this interest in the effect of the Celler-Kefauver Act, "Has the amended statute halted concentration-increasing mergers which would not have been arrested under legal doctrine prevailing prior to 1950? This is probably the most relevant test of the effectiveness of Section 7. Whatever else Congress may have had in mind when it amended that statute, it is clear from the Senate and House reports on the bill that one of its purposes was to check the rise of market concentration before it attained Sherman Act proportions."[24]

Table 1-1.   Percentage Distribution of Merger Disappearances by Type and Period of Acquisition, 1926-64.

Type of Merger	1926-1930	1940-1947	1948-1953	1954-1959	1960-1964
Horizontal	64.3	62.0	31.0	24.8	12.0
Vertical	4.8	17.0	10.3	13.7	17.0
Market Extension	11.7	a	6.9	6.4	6.9
Product Extension and Other	19.3	21.0	51.8	55.1	64.1
Total	100.0	100.0	100.0	100.0	100.0

[a]For this period Market Extension mergers are included in Horizontal.

Source: Carl Eis, "The 1919-1930 Merger Movement in American Industry," Journal of Law and Economics, (Oct. 1969), p. 294.

By the 1960s some evidence was available demonstrating that such mergers had been contained. Table 1, taken from a study by Carl Eis,[25] shows the percentage distribution of the composition of mergers from 1926 to 1964. In the two periods prior to the 1950 Amendment, well over fifty per cent of the mergers involved the acquisition of a competitor. However, following the Act's passage, the proportion of horizontal mergers to total merger activity fell from thirty-one per cent in 1948-53 to twelve per cent in 1960-64. This trend continued into the 1970s, as will be seen in chapter 2.

However, not all economists were in agreement about the effectiveness of the amended Clayton Act. Richard Posner, for example, recommends the repeal of all antitrust laws except Section 1 of the Sherman

Act. He advocates using Section 1 instead of the Celler-Kefauver Act to prevent mergers.[26]

This book provides a formal benefit-cost framework with which to effectively evaluate the success of the Celler-Kefauver Act. The existence of two conditions have set the stage for this study. The first is the careful effort of many previous researchers. The present study could not be undertaken without the identification of merger activity in the beginning part of this century by Carl Eis, the careful analyses by J. Fred Weston and Ralph Nelson examining the external conditions determining merger activity, the insight of Willard F. Mueller and Jesse Markham into the importance and role of the deterrent effect, the econometric study by Preston and Collins estimating the relationship between price-cost margins and concentration, and the methodology for measuring the benefits from antitrust developed by Leonard Weiss, to name only a few.

The second condition making this research possible is the amount of time that has transpired since the 1950 Amendment. During those thirty years, the impact of the Celler-Kefauver Act on the economy has been registered. There has been ample time permitting a researcher to gauge the response of merger activity to antitrust cases. Because of the existence of these two conditions, this study is able to actualize a vision held by many researchers shortly after the 1950 Amendment was enacted.

Chapter 2 reviews the major contributions in the antitrust literature that (1) judge the efficiency of the allocation of antitrust resources, (2) examine the effect of the Celler-Kefauver Act on the economy, and (3) identify the determinants of merger activity. In chapter 3 a formal framework for measuring the redistribution and allocative efficiency benefits is introduced. Both the direct gain from preventing the merger and the external benefits resulting from deterrence are included as benefits.

Chapter 4 undertakes an excursion into the counter-factual. It is oriented toward answering one question: "How many horizontal mergers would have occurred in the absence of the Celler-Kefauver Act and its subsequent enforcement?" This permits an estimation of the deterrent effect resulting from the 1950 Amendment.

Chapter 5 measures the cost of horizontal merger enforcement. This is based on data from the antitrust agencies, along with their institutional procedures.

Using the framework for measuring benefits developed earlier in conjunction with the estimated deterrent effect and enforcement costs, chapter 6 compares the benefits from horizontal merger enforcement with the costs. This makes possible an evaluation of the effectiveness of horizontal merger enforcement and answers the question, "Have the benefits been worth the cost to society?" Finally, in chapter 7, conclusions from this study are drawn.

2

Review of the Literature

This chapter reviews the major empirical studies relevant to this study. These papers vary considerably in scope and focus. One branch of the literature examines the relationship between the number of cases undertaken in an industry and the degree of allocative inefficiency associated with that industry. This research implicity assumes the benefit-cost ratio to be maximized if cases are brought against firms in the industries experiencing the highest profit rates and largest level of sales.

Another area of the literature tries to identify the effect of the antitrust laws on the economy. These studies are more concerned with finding relationships between antitrust activity and industry structure (along with firm behavior) than judging the manner in which the antitrust agencies allocate resources.

A major part of this study involves explaining horizontal merger activity. Therefore, the third area of literature to be reviewed includes research examining the determinants of merger activity.

The Allocation of Antitrust Resources

The first branch of literature reviewed here addresses the question: "Are the resources of the antitrust agencies employed in a manner that yields the highest social rate of return?" Richard Posner provided some insight into this question, as well as the data on the types of cases undertaken and the industries subject to antitrust enforcement that were the basis for subsequent research undertaken by several authors. In "A Statistical Analysis of Antitrust Enforcement,"[1] Posner examined violations alleged by the Department of Justice between 1890 and 1969. His results are shown in table 2-1. Posner's classification system included some double counting of cases for multiple violations, and he encountered some difficulty in categorizing complaints between monopolizing and horizontal

Table 2-1. Topical Classification of Department of Justice Antitrust Charges

	Period in Which Case Was Instituted																
	1890 to 1894	1895 to 1899	1900 to 1904	1905 to 1909	1910 to 1914	1915 to 1919	1920 to 1924	1925 to 1929	1930 to 1934	1935 to 1939	1940 to 1944	1945 to 1949	1950 to 1954	1955 to 1959	1960 to 1964	1965 to 1969	Total
Horizontal Conspiracy	3	7	5	28	62	29	50	36	19	34	179	114	122	122	104	75	989
Monopolizing	3		1	9	25	3	7	8	9	14	65	60	62	45	40	19	370
Acquisitions Short of Monopoly		1		2	3	1	1	5	1	3	2	5	3	26	61	80	194
Boycott		1		2	15	9	10	20	5	8	43	20	44	38	18	12	245
Resale Price Maintenance					2	4	2			1	1		4	4	8	2	27
Vertical Integration			2		3		1	1	2	7	6	11	6	6	7	1	53
Tying Arrangements					3	2		1	1	4	8	23	12	5	4	2	65
Exclusive Dealing	1		1	1	9	1	3	1		4	16	24	29	23	22	6	140
Territorial and Customer Limitations											8	2	4	28	24	13	74
Violence	4				2		8	3	10	7	8			4		2	47
Price Discrimination	1	1		3	6	2	1	4		5	29	20	16	15	14	6	123
Other Predatory or Unfair Conduct	1			3	2	3	1	2	1	5	27	17	7	4	11	4	88
Interlocking Directorates								2		1			4	2	2		16
Clayton Act, sec. 10													1		2		3
Labor Cases	3			2	6		16	6	7	18	35	2	17	7	5	1	125
Patent and Copyright Cases					6	1	8	3	2	3	36	45	22	15	13	11	165
Total Cases in Period	9	1	6	39	91	43	66	69	30	57	223	157	159	195	215	195	1551

Source: Richard A. Posner, "A Statistical Study of Antitrust Enforcement," p. 398.

conspiracy. All Robinson-Patman cases are excluded from the table, except those cases charging predatory price discrimination.

Posner also classified all violations alleged in Federal Trade Commission cases. Table 2-2 shows that between 1915 and 1969 the FTC has concentrated on horizontal price fixing and has given much less attention to monopolization than has the Justice Department. Posner found this preoccupation on price fixing at the FTC ". . . curious in light of its inability to impose punitive sanctions."[2]

Using this summary data of the different violations alleged in cases, Posner made several inferences about the effectiveness of the antitrust agencies. In one sample year, 1963, Posner found that of the 260 restraint-of-trade decisions at the FTC, 244 constituted violations of the Robinson-Patman Act. These cases involved allowances by manufacturers to department stores and magazine publishers to dealers. Posner observed that, "In none of these cases did the Commission suggest or is it likely that there was monopoly power at the manufacturer level or monopoly power at the distributor level of the industries involved."[3] Because these violations do not generally create or increase monopoly power, Posner concluded that the majority of FTC cases contribute little toward improving economic efficiency.

Posner also classified the antitrust cases brought by both the FTC and the Department of Justice by industry group at the two-digit Standard Industrial Classification level. He neither presented the tables due to to their "voluminous nature," nor did he completely analyze the data, although he reported that, ". . . a large proportion of the Department's cases—and an even larger percentage of the FTC's—are brought in industries not normally regarded as highly concentrated."[4] Again, Posner inferred that this allocation of antitrust resources does not greatly reduce welfare loss and therefore does not yield the highest social gain: "So far as I am able to determine, the Department of Justice, to take the most distinguished component of the antitrust enforcement system, makes little effort to identify those markets in which serious problems of monopoly are likely to arise; except in the merger area, does not act save on complaint; makes no systematic effort to see whether its decrees are complied with, . . ."[5]

Posner's 1970 study is very useful in identifying the historical record of antitrust activity. However, his evaluation of the antitrust agencies was based on observations that cases seem to be oriented toward violations that do not challenge monopoly power and that they are brought in unconcentrated industries. No measurement of actual benefits or costs from the different types of cases was presented.

Using Posner's data, William Long, Richard Schramm, and Robert

Table 2-2. Violations Alleged in FTC Cases

Violation	1915 to 1919	1920 to 1924	1925 to 1929	1930 to 1934	1935 to 1939	1940 to 1944	1945 to 1949	1950 to 1954	1955 to 1959	1960 to 1964	1960 to 1965	Grand Total	1930 to 1969 Total
Horizontal Price Fixing	11	35	9	14	74	64	26	25	22	7	4	291	236
Monopolization	3	11	3	2	10	8	1	3	1	12	6	60	43
Acquisition Short of Monopoly	17	18	18	3	18	2	1	6	22	31	51	187	134
Boycott	8	20	5	5	23	28	6	14	9	5	2	125	92
Resale Price Maintenance	62	70	21	6	14	0	2	1	9	6	6	197	44
Tying	25	17	1	2	10	15	7	7	3	2	0	89	46
Exclusive Dealing	47	24	2	4	11	5	11	11	29	7	1	152	79
Price Discrimination[a]	72	28	3	5	11	10	1	1	5	6	2	144	41
Violence	4	3	4	0	3	0	0	0	2	2	0	18	3
Labor	0	0	0	0	5	4	0	0	2	0	0	11	11
Patents	0	0	0	0	2	2	3	0	0	0	0	7	7
Other or N.A.	4	4	1	4	2	1	0	1	3	2	2	24	15
TOTAL	253	230	67	45	183	139	58	69	107	80	74	1305	751

Source: Richard A. Posner, "A Statistical Study of Antitrust Enforcement," p. 408.

Tollinson[6] employed a more traditional cost-benefit framework to analyze antitrust activity. Benefits were defined as economic efficiency (measured by the welfare triangle) and income redistribution (measured by excess profits).

Relying on a methodology introduced by Harberger[7] and measured by Kamerschen[8] and Schwartzman,[9] the value of the welfare loss, W, was equal to

$$W = 0.5(\pi /S)^2 \times S \times \eta$$

where π is excess or monopoly profits, S is total sales revenue, and η is the price elasticity of demand. Excess profits are those profits greater than the level of profits required to earn a competitive rate of return. This was somewhat arbitrarily measured as the two-digit manufacturing industry earning the lowest rate of return.

The welfare loss is comprised of two components, monopoly power and industry size. Monopoly power was measured by both the industry four-firm concentration ratio and by the rate of return on sales. Total sales revenue was used to measure size.

With a sample of cases brought by the Antitrust Division occuring within two-digit Standard Industrial Classification (SIC) manufacturing industries during the period 1945 to 1970, Long, et al., ran an ordinary least squares regression of the number of cases brought in each industry on welfare losses associated with that industry. They found that both the welfare loss and excess profits appear to play minor roles in explaining antitrust activity. However, industry size was found to be positively related with the number of cases brought in that industry.

Using the structural measure of monopoly power—the four-firm concentration ratio—Long, et al., found no statistically significant relationship between concentration and the number of cases brought against an industry. Their study suggested that industry sales are the only significant explanatory factor of antitrust activity and that profits and concentration are relatively unimportant. Therefore, they concluded that neither economic efficiency nor the redistribution of monopoly profits are the determinants of antitrust enforcement; cases are not undertaken in those industries where restructuring would yield the highest benefits.

Long, et al., also attempted to test the influence of the costs of enforcement on case selection. Although they acknowledged that the economic costs of a case include investigation and courtroom expenses, they were unable to procure such data. Instead, they substituted a surrogate variable, total industry assets, as a measure of the relative stock of economic resources available to firms in an industry for legal defense. It is expected that this proxy variable is inversely related to the number of cases brought in an industry. When this variable was included in the welfare benefit equation, Long, et al., found a negative but statistically insignificant influence on antitrust cases.

The authors did express concern about the high level of aggregation at which their empirical work was tested. Because many of the two-digit SIC industry groups are not homogeneous with respect to profit rates, concentration, and industry sales, the effect of these variables on the number of antitrust cases brought in each industry will be understated.

John Siegfried[10] attempted to correct for this aggregation problem by using less aggregated data that corresponds to IRS minor industries. This enabled regressions with observations more closely resembling a meaningful industry level than the level used in Long, et al. Even though Siegfried used a welfare loss model computed for industry classifications closer to the level of aggregation which is generally conceded to produce the most economically relevant classifications, the conclusions of Long, et al., remained unchanged. According to Siegfried, "We must conclude that economic benefits, in the form of efficiency gains and income redistributions, do not play any discernable role in the allocation of Antitrust Division resources."[11]

Peter Asch added a further dimension to the relationship between industry sales and the number of Department of Justice cases revealed in Long, et al.[12] Asch posited two hypotheses why such a relationship might exist: (1) The Antitrust Division may actively pursue cases in larger industries, and (2) the detected relationship between industry size and the number of antitrust cases is simply the result of a larger number of firms in industries with a larger volume of sales.

To test these hypotheses, Asch controlled for the fact that larger industries contain more firms and, if violations occur randomly across firms, will have a greater number of reported violations. Including variables measuring the number of firms in each industry and the average annual sales per firm in the basic regression equation used by Long, et al., produced somewhat ambiguous results. Asch found that the effect of industry size on antitrust activity is attributable both to the number of firms and to the average size of the firms within the industry.

James Meehan and Michael Mann also attempted to judge antitrust resource allocation by examining the output of the antitrust agencies over a six-year period.[13] They categorized 143 FTC cases and 112 Department of Justice cases from 1964 to 1969 by industry structure according to a classification scheme devised by Joe Bain,[14] and implemented by Clabault and Burton.[15] Unlike Long, et al., Meehan and Mann were able to analyze industries at the four-digit SIC level. Their study indicated that little antitrust attention was devoted toward highly concentrated oligopolistic industries. Only four of the 113 Department of Justice cases were in industries with four-firm concentration ratios exceeding eighty per cent. Most of the antitrust cases undertaken were in industries with four-firm concentration between nineteen per cent and sixty-five percent. Meehan and Mann interpreted this result as having implications about the benefits yielded from antitrust enforcement: ". . . most of this effort, with the exception of horizontal mergers, is of questionable merit because little or no serious economic analysis is used to demonstrate the harm of the particular practice attached to the consumer."[16]

Their study also showed a substantial portion of FTC cases involving Robinson-Patman violations which, ". . . because they more likely than not were public policy actions which hindered competition, probably had a negative return for the consumer."[17] Similarly, most of the Department of Justice price-fixing cases were in industries with moderate or low concentration where price-fixing agreements are unlikely to be unsuccessful. Meehan and Mann concluded, "What occurs, then, are zero and negative returns from these Department of Justice and FTC cases."[18]

The above studies employ a methodology of seeking out relationships between industry characteristics and the number of antitrust cases. On the basis of these relationships, and the relationships not found to exist, inferences are drawn about the appropriateness of the record of enforcement undertaken by the antitrust agencies. This approach can be criticized on several grounds.

First, most antitrust cases are filed against firms, not industries, especially at the two-digit level. These studies would consider an antitrust case against the smallest firm in an industry as having an identical effect as a case against the largest firm. That is, a complaint in a given industry would yield the same benefits, regardless of the defendant.

Similarly, with the exception of Meehan and Mann, all of these studies implicitly assume that the different types of cases are homogeneous with respect to social benefits. All cases are unambiguously considered to have the same effect. There is no differentiation among monopolization cases, price-fixing cases, Robinson-Patman cases, etc. Also, there is no provision for recognizing those cases with negative economic benefits— for example, the prohibition of a vertical merger realizing economies of scale, or a Robinson-Patman case preventing price competition. If confronted with an antitrust enforcement record consisting entirely of Robinson-Patman cases in the largest or most profitable industry, the preceding papers would seemingly conclude there was a very rational allocation of antitrust resources.

A more fundamental criticism of the framework used in these papers is that the constraints of existing antitrust law are assumed away. Structural changes resulting from monopolization cases traditionally require a court inference of intent to monopolize via abnormal business conduct. If such conduct is not easily visible, or non-existent, bringing these cases achieves only a waste of taxpayers' money and frustration at the Antitrust Division. Even if the enforcement agencies were to target specific industries, a price-fixing case cannot be brought without evidence of price-fixing; a horizontal merger case cannot be brought without the occurrence or plan of a horizontal consolidation. There may not always exist a large supply of potential cases in every industry, especially where concentration is high and firms are large.

The biggest criticism of this branch of antitrust literature is that judgments are made about the resource allocation of the enforcement agencies with only partial knowledge of the benefits yielded from cases and virtually no knowledge of the costs of undertaking these cases. Yet, one researcher was able to conclude that the antitrust agencies "are ignoring the prerequisites . . . of serious planning."[19] To make a rational economic selection of cases, the FTC and Department of Justice must consider costs as well as benefits. Even if a monopolization case against one of the largest firms in the most profitable industry is feasible, if the costs of undertaking the case are sufficiently high, the appropriate decision might easily be to initiate a different case instead, even if it involved a smaller industry.

Long, et al., included a proxy measure of enforcement costs—total industry assets—in their analysis. This variable implicitly assumed that costs are invariant among the different types of violations. The same economic cost is assigned to a price-fixing case as to a monopolization case, etc.

In summary, inferences about the economic rationale of antitrust resource allocation based on the methodology used in the previous papers cannot be readily accepted. It does not seem possible to judge case selection without considering that (1) cases against different firms in an industry yield different benefits; (2) different types of cases yield different benefits; and (3) different types of cases incur different enforcement costs and therefore different benefit-cost ratios.

The Economic Effect of Antitrust

Another section of the literature relevant to this study examines the economic effects of the various antitrust laws. These effects take the form of altering the structure of an industry, changing merger behavior, or placing constraints on certain business conduct, such as price-fixing. Studies investigating how antitrust activity influences the economy are important to this study because a major benefit of the Celler-Kefauver Act has been the deterrent effect—a reduction in the number of horizontal mergers. Thus, particular attention is devoted to the methodology used in these papers.

In "The Economic Effect of the Antitrust Laws,"[20] George J. Stigler stated that the major purpose of his study was to improve the procedures for measuring how several of the antitrust statutes altered economic behavior. He compared the experience of the United States with the record of another country with a similar type of economic system, Great Britain, which had not had an analogous public policy against the centralization of private power. Using the Herfindahl index, Stigler compared the level of concentration in seven industries over a sixty-year period between the United States and England. Stigler reported that the evidence supported the hypothesis that the Sherman Act was a modest deterrent to high concentration.

Another of the important antitrust laws was the antimerger amendment to the Clayton Act in 1950. Stigler suggested that the appropriate method for determining the effect of the Celler-Kefauver Act was to examine merger activity prior to the Act's passage with the record in subsequent years. Unfortunately, Stigler's analysis was limited to 1948 as its earliest observation. He explained: ". . . the extent of horizontal mergers in earlier times has not been measured—it seems incredible but it is true that all forms of merger are combined in the standard merger series."[21]

Jesse W. Markham also analyzed the effectiveness of the amended Clayton Act by examining the outcome of specific merger cases and comparing the legal doctrine used by the court before and after the Celler-Kefauver Amendment.[22] Markham found that mergers which were allowed by the courts under the Sherman Act would most likely have been found in violation of the amended Clayton Act:

> There can be little doubt that through application of these standards the new Section 7 arrested several dozen mergers that would easily have passed muster prior to 1950. This point was emphasized by the Federal Trade Commission in its Pillsbury (50 FTC 55) opinion, the Commission's first interpretation of the amended Section 7 in the context of a specific merger case. In declaring Pillsbury's two acquisitions, Ballard, and Ballard and Duff, in contravention to Section 7 the Commission sought to clarify the standards it employed. In doing so it observed that the merger in *U.S. v. Columbia Steel Co.* (334 U.S. 495) which safely passed the Sherman Act tests of legality two years before Section 7 was amended, would probably have been declared illegal under the tests laid down in Pillsbury.[23]

Willard F. Mueller, in a study prepared for the Judiciary Committee of Congress,[24] examined both the effects of merger activity and the record of merger enforcement from 1951 to 1977. Table 2-3, taken from Mueller's

Table 2-3.   Percentage Distribution of Large Acquisitions Challenged in Mining and Manufacturing, By Type of Merger, 1951-77

Type of Merger Challenged	1951–55		1956–60		1961–65		1966–70		1971–77		Total, 1951–77	
	Number	Assets	Number	Assets	Number	Assets	Number	Assets	Number	Assets	Number	Assets
Horizontal	33	29	58	68	64	76	65	64	72	53	62	65
Vertical	33	38	30	27	19	6	10	1	7	6	18	7
Conglomerate	33	32	13	5	17	17	25	34	20	42	20	29
Market Extension	20	20	5	1	4	1	6	5	0	0	6	5
Product Extension	13	12	8	4	11	5	15	6	17	41	12	13
Other	0	0	0	0	2	11	4	23	3	1	2	11
Total	100	100	100	100	100	100	100	100	100	100	100	100

Source: Willard F. Mueller, "The Celler-Kefauver Act: The First 27 Years," p. 16.

report, shows that the majority of merger enforcements, measured both in terms of number of firms and assets involved, have been oriented toward horizontal mergers. Only during the 1951-55 period were less than fifty per cent of the large acquisitions challenged in the category of horizontal consolidations.

What was the result of this merger enforcement? Mueller observed, "Although there are notable divestitures, the chief impact of merger policy is the deterrent effect of threatened prosecution. This aspect of enforcement policy is most evident in the area of horizontal mergers, where the legal rules became increasingly clearer after 1956-58."[25]

Table 2-4 shows the composition of large acquisitions in manufacturing and mining from 1951 to 1977. Horizontal mergers comprised about thirty-four per cent of the number of large acquisitions in the five years immediately following the Celler-Kefauver Act. The proportion of horizontal mergers relative to total merger activity declined into the early 1960s. By 1966 to 1970, during the peak of the merger wave, only nine per cent of the number of mergers were horizontal.

Mueller also examined the effect of enforcement in seven different industries. For example, in dairy processing, merger activity by the largest firms was reduced after the FTC initiated four complaints. After 1962, when the Commission announced its first decision which included guidelines for dairy processing mergers, the eight largest companies ended almost all dairy processing acquisitions.

From his industry investigations, Mueller concluded:

These case studies illustrate that usually the most important impact of merger enforcement policy is deterrence. For example, in the first 12 months following the initial

Table 2-4. Large Acquisitions (Actual and Proposed) in Manufacturing and Mining, By Type of Merger, 1951-77

Type of Merger	1951-55		1956-60		1961-65		1966-70		1971-77		Total	
	Number	Assets	Number	Assets	Number	Assets	Number	Assets	Number	Assets	Number	Assets
Horizontal	52	$1,900	65	$3,107	62	$3,105	59	$6,554	115	$6,878	353	$21,454
Vertical	20	628	36	1,322	51	2,554	52	2,431	32	1,852	191	8,787
Conglomerate	82	2,473	156	4,384	212	8,334	529	35,580	346	24,764	1,325	75,526
Product Extension	55	1,811	97	2,690	143	4,664	329	16,683	162	8,223	786	34,071
Market Extension	7	127	18	429	16	1,365	18	2,962	22	1,673	81	6,556
Other	20	535	41	1,265	53	2,305	182	15,935	162	14,858	458	34,898
Total	154	5,001	257	8,813	325	13,903	640	44,565	493	33,84	1,869	105,766
	Percentage distribution by type of merger											
Horizontal	34	38	25	35	19	22	9	15	23	21	19	20
Vertical	13	13	14	15	16	18	8	5	7	6	10	9
Conglomerate	53	49	61	50	65	60	83	80	70	73	71	71
Product Extension	36	36	38	31	44	33	51	37	33	24	42	32
Market Extension	4	2	7	5	5	10	3	7	4	5	4	6
Other	13	11	16	14	16	17	29	36	33	44	25	33
Total	100	100	100	100	100	100	100	100	100	100	100	100

Source: Willard F. Mueller, "The Celler-Kefauver Act: The First 27 Years," p. 20.

decision dismissing the National Tea Case, the 10 largest food chains made market-extension acquisitions of firms with total sales of over $500 million. This was greater than all such acquisitions challenged to that date by the Commission. And were it not for the enforcement policy subsequently applied to the industry, the largest chains almost certainly would have continued to be leading acquirers. Similarly, were it not for the FTC's enforcement policy toward mergers in the dairy industry, the eight largest dairies may well have acquired hundreds of dairies since 1960. The record in banking is equally dramatic where enforcement has virtually stopped all significant horizontal mergers.[26]

While Mueller's study was more concerned with the mergers that never occurred, as a result of the deterrent effect, Kenneth G. Elzinga's paper[27] examined the relief obtained by the government in cases prohibiting a merger. Using a sample of thirty-nine cases, Elzinga categorized the decisions over a continuum of the degree of success of the relief. His basis for success was (1) independence of the new firm from the acquiring firm, (2) viability of the new firm, and (3) the time required to reestablish the independent, visible firm. Of the thirty-nine cases, twenty-one relief orders were not considered successful.

Elzinga introduced his study with the premise that an effective antimerger statute requires effective relief. However, even if the majority of cases have not been subject to effective divestiture, as Elzinga found, the Celler-Kefauver Act still has had a considerable impact through deterrence, as made clear in Mueller's study.

These studies show several dimensions of the impact of antitrust enforcement. Stigler compared the level of concentration, measured by the Herfindahl index, between the United States and Great Britain; Mueller examined the shift in the composition of merger activity, interpreted as a result of deterrence from Celler-Kefauver enforcement; and Elzinga investigated the effectiveness of the remedies provided in the cases won by the government. None of these papers, however, attempted to actually measure the benefits from antitrust policy and compare them with the cost of enforcement. Such a study is desirable, according to Markham, because, "The effectiveness of any investment of public policy must be assessed in terms of how closely the results directly attributable to the policy conform to those it clearly seeks to achieve. When both the objectives and the results can be quantitatively defined, such assessments can be conclusive."[28]

The only major study presenting a benefit-cost framework for analyzing the allocation of antitrust resources was undertaken by Leonard W. Weiss.[29] Based on apparent Congressional intent, Weiss believes the major benefit of antitrust is the redistribution of wealth from firms with monopoly power to consumers. A secondary benefit, emphasized primarily by economists, is allocative efficiency.

Weiss assigned a different level of benefits to each of ten types of antitrust cases. The amount of benefits depends upon (1) the direct gain to consumers as a share of the defendant's annual sales, (2) the estimated duration of effect, and (3) the number of cases of the same size prevented by a successful case.

The direct gains from each violation were empirically based. For example, the direct gain from a criminal collusion case was derived from the elevation of prices in the electrical equipment cases, the Seattle bread conspiracy, and the bleachers' conspiracy. A horizontal merger case prevents an increase in the market share of the acquiring firm. Numerous studies have found a positive relation between the price-cost margin and the four-firm concentration ratio. Taking this empirical relationship as given, Weiss showed that an increase in concentration resulting from a merger led to an increase in the price-cost margin. The gain to consumers from preventing the merger was found to be proportional to the size of the acquired firm.

There is less evidence available for estimating the magnitude of the deterrent effect. Weiss assumed that the deterrence from a case is proportional to its size because the publicity for non-precedent cases is most likely directly related to the size of the case. This framework also recognizes negative externalities from cases. Structural monopoly cases were assigned a mildly negative side effect because other dominant firms may perceive such a case as a signal to compete less vigorously.

Multiplying the gain from each type of case by the probability of success yielded the expected value of estimated consumer gain per dollar of sales. Weiss obtained measures of the probability of success from interviews with the administrators responsible for enforcement of antitrust activities at the Antitrust Division. All settlements were considered a success, although this is not likely to be always true, especially in structural monopoly cases.

In his interviews, Weiss also inquired about the number of Antitrust Division full-time attorney years expended on the average case for each type of violation. He was able to weight the costs for the differential in lawyer-years between pre-trial settlements and completed trials. Not only did his estimates exclude the costs of appeals, legislation, consultation with agencies, and internal administration, but also the costs of investigations that never resulted in a complaint. To accommodate these excluded costs, Weiss tripled the direct lawyer-years per case. Based on the number of antitrust practitioners registered in the American Bar Association, Section of Antitrust, relative to the number of government attorneys engaged in antitrust enforcement, it was estimated that five private attorney-years are expended for each government attorney-year.

The expected gain per Antitrust Division lawyer-year was obtained by multiplying the mean sales for each type of complaint by the expected consumer gain per dollar of sales and dividing by the estimated full-time lawyer-years expended.

This framework made possible a comparison of benefits with costs for each of the ten selected categories, and therefore provided a means for evaluating the allocation of antitrust resources. Weiss qualified his findings by observing that this procedure was essentially static—no insight was gained into the rate at which the benefit-cost ratios change as additional cases are undertaken. There was no estimate or incorporation of diminishing returns in his analysis. Similarly, no attempt or method was suggested to evaluate precedent cases. It can be expected that deterrence from these cases is especially important.

The Determinants of Merger Activity

The third branch of the literature under review examines studies that try to explain merger activity. This is relevant to this study because in measuring the deterrent effect resulting from Celler-Kefauver enforcement, a model for predicting large horizontal mergers will be estimated. No previous research has ever been concerned with explaining only one type of merger—horizontal. However, previous studies do reveal which economic variables are most likely to be related to merger activity in general.

Peter Steiner makes a distinction between studies that examine principal-cause and multiple-cause hypotheses.[30] The principal-cause hypotheses identify the motivations causing mergers and include these variables, or their proxy representations, in an econometric model. The multiple-cause hypotheses try to find significant relationships between merger activity and key variables reflecting the general economic climate.

In a paper which Steiner would place in the principal-cause category, Stanley E. Boyle tested the hypothesis that mergers occur to rectify disequilibria between firm profit rates.[31] For the period 1948 to 1968, Boyle selected 698 of the 1,275 acquired firms for which financial data was available for the five years prior to the merger. He found that few firms were unprofitable and that the average profit rate for the acquired firms was only slightly less than that of all firms. Boyle rejected the theory that mergers are a kind of arbitrage to adjust for differences in firm profit rates.

Boyles' paper was substantiated by the *Economic Report on Conglomerate Merger Performance, An Empirical Analysis of Nine Corporations,* a study undertaken by the FTC.[32] Examining the firms acquired by nine conglomerates over a one-year period, it was found that almost none of the purchased firms were unprofitable in the year prior to acquisition. There was, however, a slight difference in the degree of profitability between the acquiring and the acquired firms. The paper did find that the average size of the acquired firm seemed to vary considerably over a nine-year period. From 1960 to 1969 the average size of purchased companies was about $28 million. The average size of the 194 acquisitions that occurred between 1960 and 1965 was $9.6 million. This was a large contrast to the 1966-67 period when the average size was $23.7 million for the eighty-five acquisitions taking place. In 1968 there were sixty-nine mergers with an average size of $84.5 million. The average size of the acquired company does seem to follow the merger wave of the 1960s fairly closely.

Samuel R. Reid tested the hypothesis that management-controlled firms, as measured by growth variables, have a larger propensity to merge.[33] Reid classified 478 of the largest 500 firms in 1961 by the amount of merger activity for the period 1951 to 1961. He found that the higher the level of merger activity, the more likely were the growth variables to be at high levels. Growth was measured by changes in sales, changes in assets, and changes in employees. Reid also found that merger activity was inversely related to variables measuring firm profitability.

The results of a paper by Thomas F. Hogarty conflicted somewhat with Reid's conclusion.[34] For the 1953-1964 period, Hogarty assembled a sample of forty-three firms that had acquired through merger assets of at least twenty per cent of the pre-merger level. The sample, therefore, consisted of firms experiencing intense acquisition records. He compared the performance of each firm in his sample with the rest of the firm's industry. Examining stock prices and dividend policies, Hogarty found that most firms had a stock market performance similar to that of their industry, but with a greater variance.

The preceding papers are of a principal-cause nature. They hypothesize one cause of merger activity and then undertake statistical analyses to test that hypothesis. The primary goal of this study is not to isolate *the* most important motivation that induces mergers; rather, it is to explain the aggregate level of horizontal merger activity. Because of one question addressed in this study—how many large horizontal mergers would have occurred annually in the absence of merger enforcement—Steiner's multiple-cause approach is more appropriate for the analysis adapted here. It is less important for this study to identify an exact causal relationship between mergers and the motivations enticing firms to merge, than to model the relationship between merger activity and external economic conditions.

Steiner supports the multiple-cause model: "To be sure it does not seem possible to find definitive support for a principal cause of merger activity, but remembering that a merger wave is an aggregate of many mergers, there is substantial support in these data and in the historical experience taken as a whole for a motivation model."[35]

Steiner explains why multiple-cause models are not inconsistent with principal-cause models, but may be more useful, given the data constraints in predicting merger activity:

> Suppose that certain motivations are always present with respect to some potential mergers. These would include opportunities for real economies, for increased profits via market power, for settling intracorporate fights, for achieving growth objectives, and for earning commissions on the exchange of securities. Let me postulate that these are important motivations and that while they may become stronger or weaker in response to exogenous influences, they are always there to a significant degree. For any level of other variables, they would always motivate some mergers. But the more conducive other considerations become, the more mergers actually get consummated. It takes mutual benefits to make a merger. If the stock market suddenly becomes bullish toward mergers, a merger that managers always wanted (but owners resisted) may become attractive to the owners of the target company. If credit conditions tighten and interest rates rise, the advantage of acquiring idle liquid assets and transferring them tax free, may be the straw that motivates a merger that previously had latent market power advantages which were, however, not by themselves worth the antitrust risk.[36]

One of the earliest studies explaining total merger activity using regression analysis was undertaken by J. Fred Weston.[37] Weston used a sample of seventy-four firms for the period 1920 to 1938. One of his primary interests was how the timing of the merger wave compared to the timing of the business cycle. The average peak in merger activity was found to lag two-thirds of a quarter behind the relevant peak of the reference business cycle. The average trough of merger activity lagged four quarters behind the trough of the reference cycle. Based on this observed relationship between the business cycle and merger activity, Weston estimated a model explaining the total number of mergers each year. The industrial production index, the Dow Jones Price Index, and the wholesale price index were used as explanatory variables. Only the stock price index and wholesale price index proved to be statistically significant. Weston's study is useful because it identifies the business cycle, and therefore variables correlated with the business cycle, such as stock prices and the price level, as reliable predictors of merger activity.

The relationships between merger acitivity and stock prices, and between mergers and industrial production were also examined by Ralph L. Nelson.[38] Using the annual number of firm disappearances from 1895 to 1954 as his measure of merger activity, Nelson calculated a simple correlation of .469 between mergers and the Dow Jones Industrial Stock Price Index, and a correlation of .0470 between merger activity and industrial production.

Nelson also tested for the existence of short-run relationships. Dividing his sample into five subperiods, he found a statistically significant correlation coefficient, at the five per cent level of significance, between stock prices and merger activity in all of the periods, except during the Depression years 1932 to 1942. However, in only two of the periods, 1905 to 1918 and 1919 to 1931, was there a statistically significant correlation between industrial production and mergers. And, in the last two periods, 1932 to 1942 and 1943 to 1954, Nelson actually found a negative correlation between mergers and industrial production.

Based on his analysis, Nelson concluded that there is a strong relationship between merger activity and stock prices, but the existence of a relationship between mergers and industrial production is dubious: ". . . mergers were more positively correlated to stock-price changes than to changes in industrial production in the three periods of high merger activity—1895-1904, 1919-1931, and 1943-1954. Conversely, in the two periods of low merger activity, 1905-1919 and 1932-1942, industrial production exhibited a higher positive (or lesser negative) relationship to mergers than stock prices did. This suggests that capital market conditions or their underlying causes were of leading importance in periods of high merger activity, and that their role in times of low merger activity was not important. While industrial production was the more important factor in times of low merger activity, the correlations were so low that no strong cause-and-effect connection is suggested."[39]

Michael Gort also used a multiple-cause model to test for the determinants of merger activity.[40] Gort hypothesized two reasons why the buyers and sellers of a firm may expect an increase in wealth as a result of a merger. First, the market value of the assets of the combined firms may increase. Second, the buyer and seller may have different valuations of the acquired firm. Therefore, Gort tested to see if mergers are related to (1) economic disturbances leading to discrepancies in firm valuation; (2) monopoly motives; and (3) economies of scale.

Gort's explanatory variables consisted of technical personnel ratio, 1950; rate of change in productivity, 1947-54; growth in index of production, 1947-54; four-firm concentration ratio, 1954; change in four-firm concentration ratio, 1947-54; rate of change in average firm asset size, 1948-54; and rate of change in the number of firms and proprietors, 1947-54.

Using the period 1951 to 1959, Gort's sample consisted of 5,534 acquisitions among manufacturing firms, with a cutoff size of $500,000. He classified the industry of the acquired firm at the 3-digit level. Gort found the technical personnel ratio, the productivity change, the growth variable, and the concentration ratio all to be strongly correlated with merger rates.

William N. Leonard[41] tried to account for merger activity at the two-digit SIC industry level. Leonard constructed an index of merger activity defined as the value of assets acquired in all types of mergers in each two-digit industry as of December 1959. The index was regressed against other variables indicative of market structure and performance. Leonard hypothesized that the industry groups showing the greatest merger activity would be associated with large-scale economies, high advertising intensity, high profitability, and high rates of asset growth. Leonard also expected more merger activity in the less-concentrated industries due to deterrence provided by the antitrust laws.

Leonard included the following as explanatory variables: size, scale economies, advertising intensity, profitability, rate of growth of assets, seller concentration, and research and development intensity. Of these variables, scale economies and research and development intensity had significant effects at the ninety-nine per cent confidence level; advertising intensity, profitability, and the rate of growth of total assets had insignificant effects at the ninety-five per cent confidence level.

Alan R. Beckenstein[42] used the large merger series published by the FTC to explain merger activity between 1948 and 1975. Several models were estimated, with both the number of mergers and the value of acquired assets as dependent variables measuring merger activity. Beckenstein found the prime rate and the stock price index were statistically significant explanatory variables, while GNP and changes in GNP were not. An index of antitrust litigation of merger cases during the previous year was originally included as an explanatory variable, but had so little statistical effect in explaining merger activity that it was dropped from the regression equation and not reported in the article.

The failure of this antitrust variable is not surprising since Beckenstein was trying to explain variations in all types of mergers, while merger cases have been largely oriented toward, and successful almost exclusively at, deterring horizontal and vertical mergers. In fact, it is conceivable that firms substituted non-horizontal types of mergers for horizontal acquisitions following the establishment of a clear and enforceable Celler-Kefauver Act. This might be particularly true with conglomerate mergers, since they are least vulnerable to the antitrust agencies. Therefore, antitrust enforcement may have a significant effect on horizontal and vertical merger activity, while having no influence on the total number of mergers.

3

A Framework for Benefit Estimation

Introduction

In chapter 1 the major goal of antitrust policy, as inferred from Congressional intent, was identified as the prevention of a redistribution of wealth from consumers to firms as the result of monopoly power. A secondary goal, emanating from neoclassical economic theory, is allocative efficiency. Based on these social and economic values, this chapter establishes a benefit-cost framework, which will later enable an evaluation of the economic efficiency of the Celler-Kefauver Act and its subsequent enforcement.

Such a framework provides a basis for answering two types of questions. The first type considers the effectiveness of the historical record of horizontal merger enforcement: "Has the amount of resources invested by the antitrust agencies yielded a sufficient rate of return?" The second type examines how the antitrust agencies can make the best use of their limited resources: "Given a level of horizontal merger activity, should antitrust enforcement be expanded or contracted?"

Why do certain horizontal mergers cause a redistribution of wealth and deadweight loss? One explanation is based on the evidence from numerous studies relating firm or industry profitability to market concentration. According to Leonard W. Weiss, "The concentration-profits relationship has been one of the most thoroughly tested hypotheses in economics."[1] From his exhaustive review of this branch of literature, Weiss summarizes, "The bulk of the studies show a significant positive effect of concentration on profit margins."[2]

One type of concentration-profits study uses the four-firm concentration ratio to explain price-cost margins. The four-firm concentration ratio is the share of the market accounted for by the four largest firms, and the price-cost margin approximates the difference between price and marginal cost, divided by price. For example, in a paper by Norman

Collins and Lee Preston,[3] a significant positive relationship was found between the price-cost margin and the four-firm concentration ratio. This result has implications for horizontal mergers. An acquisition or consolidation by one of the four largest firms in an industry implies an increase in the four-firm concentration ratio and a subsequent increase in the price-cost margin. This represents a transfer of wealth from consumers to firms and a reduction in allocative efficiency. Prohibition of such a merger prevents the distributive effect and deadweight loss.

Horizontal merger cases also provide indirect benefits resulting from acquisitions deterred because of antitrust enforcement. Two different methods of estimating the deterrent effect are introduced. The first procedure estimates a model explaining horizontal mergers increasing the four-firm concentration ratio over a pre-Celler-Kefauver enforcement period. The number of such mergers which would have occurred in the absence of antitrust enforcement during the ensuing years is predicted by extrapolating from the historical values of the explanatory variables. The residual between predicted and actual merger activity is then attributed to deterrence.

The second method includes variables representing antitrust enforcement in a model from 1919 to 1976 estimating merger activity. Mergers in the absence of antitrust are predicted by assigning these variables a value of zero. Deterrence is then measured by the difference between predicted and actual merger activity.

Unlike the benefits, which are based on economic theory, the cost of undertaking a horizontal merger case is identified by examining the institutional procedures at the antitrust agencies. Thus, the methodology for obtaining cost estimates will be discussed separately in chapter 5.

Benefit-Cost Framework

Based on the net present value method discussed by Sassone and Schaffer,[4] the relationship between the benefits and costs of a horizontal merger case can be represented as

$$NPV = \sum_{n=0}^{N} \frac{(B_f + \alpha\, B_q)_n}{(1 + d)^n} - \sum_{n=0}^{N} \frac{(C_a + C_p)_n}{(1 + d)^n} \qquad (3\text{-}1)$$

or

$$NPV = \sum_{n=0}^{N} \frac{(B_f)_n}{(1 + d)^n} + \alpha \sum_{n=0}^{N} \frac{(B_q)_n}{(1 + d)^n} - \sum_{n=0}^{N} \frac{(C_a + C_p)_n}{(1 + d)^n} \qquad (3\text{-}2)$$

where

B_f = allocative efficiency benefit
B_q = wealth redistribution benefit
α = subjective weighted value of one dollar of wealth redistributed
C_a = agency cost of undertaking case
C_p = private costs incurred in case
N = duration of effect
d = discount rate

Equations 3-1 and 3-2 transform a stream of future benefits and costs into an equivalent net present value. Based on these equations the benefit cost ratio, B/C, can be formed

$$B/C = \sum_{n=0}^{N} \frac{(B_f + \alpha B_q)_n}{(1 + d)^n} \bigg/ \sum_{n=0}^{N} \frac{(C_a + C_p)_n}{(1 + d)^n} \tag{3-3}$$

On what criteria should the benefit-cost ratios be evaluated? Theoretically, according to Musgrave and Musgrave,[5] evaluation should be based on the comparison with alternative public projects of either the marginal benefits from the last dollar spent on the project, or the benefit-cost ratios, depending upon the lumpiness of the projects. Since this study is limited to analyzing only one of the many antitrust laws, comparison of benefit-cost ratios with all alternative government projects is unthinkable. Therefore, a standard of sufficiency for gauging the economic efficiency of a case will be used throughout the remainder of this book. A case is considered not to be wasting public resources, and in fact, is earning a positive net social return if the benefit-cost ratio exceeds unity. Thus, a horizontal merger case is considered successful if the benefits exceed the costs. Future research may provide insight into the optimal allocation of antitrust resources among the different types of violations.

The Redistribution of Wealth

Direct Effect

The direct gain from a horizontal merger case is empirically derived from the previously mentioned plethora of research relating price-cost margins to the four-firm concentration ratio. In the Preston and Collins study the relationship between the price-cost margin and concentration ratio (excluding the other variables) took the form

$$\frac{VS - CM - W}{VS} = a + bCR_4 \tag{3-4}$$

where VS is the value of shipments, CM is the cost of materials, W is the wage cost, and CR_4 is the four-firm concentration ratio. As shown in figure 3-1, the price-cost margin measures the degree to which price is elevated above marginal cost. A horizontal merger will, according to equation 3-4, cause a subsequent rise in the price-cost margin. Since the price-cost margin is defined, in terms of figure 3-1, as

$$\left(\frac{VS - MC}{VS}\right)_1 = \frac{(p_1 \cdot q_1) - (c \cdot q_1)}{(p_1 \cdot q_1)} \tag{3-5}$$

where c is unit cost, a merger causing an increase in concentration will have the effect of raising the price-cost margin to

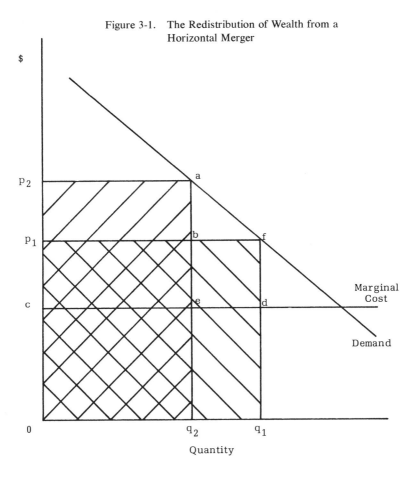

Figure 3-1.   The Redistribution of Wealth from a Horizontal Merger

$$\left(\frac{VS - MC}{VS}\right)_2 = \frac{(p_2 \cdot q_2) - (c \cdot q_2)}{(p_2 \cdot q_2)} \tag{3-6}$$

where

$$\left(\frac{VS - MC}{VS}\right)_2 > \left(\frac{VS - MC}{VS}\right)_1$$

As a result of the horizontal merger and the ensuing rise in the price-cost margin, there is a redistribution of wealth from consumers to firms, shown in figure 3-1 as $(p_1 \, bap_2) - (edfb)$. Preventing such an acquisition avoids this distributive effect.

Following a procedure used by Weiss,[6] the direct gain from a merger can also be derived algebraically from equation 3-4. If the acquiring firm is among the largest four in the industry, a merger will increase concentration by

$$\Delta \, CR_4 = \frac{VS_a}{VS}$$

where VS_a is the value of shipments of the acquired firm. Since

$$b \cdot CR_4 = b \cdot \frac{VS_a}{VS}$$

it follows that

$$\frac{\Delta \, (VS - CM - W)}{VS} = b \cdot \frac{VS_a}{VS} \cdot$$

By prohibiting a merger, the gain to consumers is

$$\Delta \, (VS - CM - W) = b \cdot VS_a \tag{3-7}$$

The benefit to consumers must be adjusted by three factors. First, the distributive effect shown in figure 3-1 applies only to a firm's net income after taxes. The tax revenues could, theoretically at least, be returned to consumers, nullifying part of the redistribution. Besides, although there is ample evidence suggesting that Congress placed a high value on preventing wealth flowing from consumers to firms as a result of monopoly power, no such Congressional concern was registered regarding a similar transfer from consumers to the public sector. Thus, only the share of VS_a representing net income accrues a direct benefit.

Similarly, no direct gain from preventing a merger exists until the divestiture of the acquired firm, or an equivalent remedy, occurs. Such relief is not usually simultaneous with a favorable court decision (from the government's perspective). In his paper discussed in the previous chapter, Kenneth Elzinga[7] found that of the merger cases occurring between 1950 and 1960, many did not obtain effective relief because of the prolonged duration required to achieve divestiture. Clearly, if a merger causes a redistribution of wealth because it increases the market concentration, and therefore the price-cost margin, the redistribution will not cease until the source of the effect—the increased concentration resulting from the merger—is eliminated. Thus, a merger case may be filed in period n, but no direct gain is accrued until obtaining effective relief. Direct benefits are zero until that time.

The direct gain measured by equation 3-7 occurs over N future years. But this annual flow of benefits must be adjusted to reflect the valuation of future benefits in the period in which the case is undertaken. Thus, the direct gain in each future year must be discounted to calculate the net present value.

Adjusting equation 3-7 for these three qualifications yields the net direct benefits from the redistribution of wealth, B_{qd},

$$B_{qd} = \sum_{n=0}^{N} \frac{(1 - tr)}{(1 + d)^n} \cdot b \cdot VS_a \cdot V_n \qquad (3-8)$$

where tr is the corporate tax rate of forty-eight percent, and b, which was estimated in the study by Preston and Collins, is 0.144. V_n is included to represent the period in which effective relief is procured. If n^* is the year of divestiture, then $V_n = 0$ for $n < n^*$, and $V_n = 1$ for $n \geq n^*$. That is, there is no direct gain from a horizontal merger case until relief has been achieved.

Although Preston and Collins undertook their study at the four-digit Standard Industrial Classification (SIC) industry level, the relationship between the four-firm concentration ratio and the price-cost margin, represented by b, is assumed to be identical for both narrower and, in a few cases, broader markets.

In most of the cases the court defines the product market at a level more similar to a five-digit industry than to a four-digit industry. For example, in the 1956 complaint against *Scovill Manufacturing Co.*, the product market was defined as "safety and common pins."[8] In this narrow line of commerce, Scovill was the leading manufacturer in the nation.

Thus, the merger increased the share of the market held by the four largest firms.

Indirect Effect

Alternative Measures of Deterrence. A horizontal merger case not only provides the direct gain measured by equation 3-8, but also provides an indirect benefit because future acquisitions do not occur as a result of the case. This is known as the deterrent effect. Deterrence from a horizontal merger case is defined as mergers that would have occurred in the absence of that particular case. Why are some plans for acquisitions and consolidations abandoned by firms because of an antitrust case? There are two major determinants of deterrence. The first is the precedent value of the case. Landes and Posner define a precedent as "something done in the past that is appealed to as a reason for doing the same thing again. . . . The earlier decision provides a reason for deciding a subsequent similar case the same way, and a series of related precedents may crystallize a rule having almost the same impact as a statutory rule."[9]

The precedent case often defines specific legal rules more clearly than the vague general norms of conduct passed into law by Congress. If the case establishes a clear legal precedent, firms will be discouraged from entering into similar contracts and conduct determined to be illegal in that case. For example, *Trenton Potteries*[10] established legal precedence because the Supreme Court asserted all fixed prices to be unreasonable, i.e., price-fixing is illegal per se. Presumably the *Trenton Potteries* decision had a considerable impact on the future conduct and contractual agreements between firms.

The second determinant of deterrence is the intensity of enforcement of existing precedents. Without subsequent enforcement, the deterrence resulting from a precedent case diminishes. There are two reasons for this. First, a case may clearly establish legal precedence, but unless future violations are prosecuted by the enforcement agencies, firms will have no reason to alter their behavior. A precedent case may clearly define an action as illegal. But it is the ensuing litigation that indicates to firms the probability of remaining unscathed if that action is undertaken. The second reason is that enforcement following a precedent case may broaden the scope of that precedent. A precedent tends to diminish in value over time because of a decline in relevance due to a changing social, economic, and judicial environment. However, the more general a precedent is, the slower is its loss in value over time.[11] Hence, the greater the intensity of enforcement of existing precedents, the greater will be the scope of those precedents, implying a larger deterrent effect.

These two determinants of deterrence—precedent value and enforcement—are interdependent. Not only does deterrence from a precedent case diminish without litigation to reinforce the precedent, but the prosecution will seem random without an established precedent. The claim is often made that enforcement of Sherman Act, Section Two cases—intent to monopolize—provides little deterrence since a clear precedent case is lacking. Because the court has adopted a rule of reason, the legality of each case is determined on a case-by-case basis; any one case probably does not affect the behavior of other firms very much. Willard F. Mueller has described the result from establishing and enforcing a clear legal precedent: ". . . we may expect, as a general rule that the chief impact of enforcement policy results from the establishment of rules of law which guide business decision-making. Hence, enforcement policy may affect a particular industry's structure even though there have been no legal actions in the industry."[12]

In a benefit-cost analysis the ideal measure of deterrence answers the question, "What would have been the effect on future mergers if this particular case had not been undertaken?" The difficulty with this approach is that the amount of deterrence from any single case—the *marginal deterrence*—is not independent of other cases brought by the antitrust agencies. The precedent value of any given case, such as *Brown Shoe*,[13] is probably positively related to the level of enforcement following the decision. Similarly, a case following the *Brown Shoe* decision may provide deterrent benefits because it reinforces the precedent set forth by the court; without the establishment of a clear-cut precedent, the case might appear to be an example of random prosecution and provide little deterrence.

Because of the interdependence between the precedent value of a case and subsequent enforcement, marginal deterrence is difficult to measure and may not identify the true amount of deterrence resulting from a case. Given the fact that deterrence from one case is contingent on future enforcement and/or previous precedents, the relevant question becomes, "What would have been the effect on future horizontal mergers if the particular bundle of cases undertaken by the antitrust agencies had not occurred?" This implies deterrence should be measured as the product of the entire enforcement bundle undertaken by the Justice Department and FTC. A measure of *average deterrence* can be obtained by dividing total deterrence by the number of cases.

The advantage of the average deterrence measure is that it recognizes the mutual interdependence of cases and attributes deterrence to the entire record of horizontal merger enforcement. However, this measure is unrealistic in the sense that all cases do not contribute equally to discouraging future mergers; surely *Brown Shoe* and *Von's Grocery*[14] discouraged more future acquisitions and consolidations than, for example, the *Hat Corp. of America* case in the hat manufacturing industry. An inherent weakness of the average deterrence measure is the assumption that deterrence is invariant among all horizontal merger cases.

Because average deterrence ignores differences in the impact of individual cases, and marginal deterrence ignores the interdependence among cases, a modified measure combining the concepts of marginal and average deterrence is developed in the following section. Two different procedures are used to estimate the number of mergers deterred by the enforcement of the Celler-Kefauver Act. The first method follows a methodology suggested by George J. Stigler.[15] To determine the effect of the Celler-Kefauver Amendment on merger activity, Stigler suggests comparing merger activity before and after 1950, and attributing the difference to antitrust policy.

The second method includes variables representing antitrust enforcement in a model explaining merger activity. By assigning these variables a value of zero, the number of mergers that would have occurred in the absence of Celler-Kefauver enforcement can be predicted. Deterrence is then measured as the difference between predicted and actual merger activity.

Method 1 for Estimating Deterrence. This method estimates a model explaining merger activity prior to effective enforcement of the Celler-Kefauver Act. An implicit assumption is that the structure of the estimated model—the relationship between the explanatory and dependent variables—would not have changed during the subsequent years had there been no Celler-Kefauver Act. This model takes the general linear form

$$M_t = \alpha + \beta_1 X_{1_t} + \beta_2 X_{2_t} + \ldots + \beta_z X_{z_t} \tag{3-9}$$

where $X_1, X_2, \ldots, X_z$ represent the selected explanatory variables, and M is the number of horizontal mergers increasing the four-firm concentration ratio. Candidates for $X_1, X_2, \ldots, X_z$, include those variables identified in the previous chapter as historically being associated with merger activity.

The regression is estimated for the period 1919-t*, where t* represents the year prior to effective Celler-Kefauver enforcement. The number of horizontal mergers increasing the four-firm concentration ratio in period t* + 1 is predicted by substituting the observed values of $X_1, X_2, \ldots, X_z$, into equation 3-9 and extrapolating the value for M_{t*+1}. That is:

$$M'_{t*+1} = \alpha + \beta_1 X_{1_{t*+1}} + \beta_2 X_{2_{t*+1}} + \ldots + \beta_z X_{z_{t*+1}}$$

where M'_{t^*+1} is the predicted value of merger activity in period $t^* + 1$.

Deterrence in period $t^* + 1$ is then measured as the residual between what merger activity would have been in the absence of antitrust enforcement and the historical value of merger activity. Thus,

$$MD_{t^*+1} = M'_{t^*+1} - M_{t^*+1}$$

Repeating this procedure for every year following t^* enables an estimate of the total amount of deterrence occurring as a result of the 1950 amendment and its subsequent enforcement. A measure of average deterrence per case, $\overline{MD}$, is obtained by dividing the total amount of deterrence over the entire period by the number of horizontal merger cases won by the government, MC. This can be represented by

$$\overline{MD} = \sum_{t^*+1}^{T} \overline{MD}_t / \sum_{t^*+1}^{T} MC_t$$

where T is the final period of extrapolation. Thus $\overline{MD}$ approximates the average number of mergers deterred by each successful horizontal merger case.

Method 2 for Estimating Deterrence. The reliability of MD determined by the previous procedure depends crucially upon the assumption that the estimated relationship between the explanatory variables and merger activity would have remained unchanged without the presence of Celler-Kefauver enforcement. Therefore, a second method is introduced that avoids such an assumption. A model explaining merger activity is again estimated, but in method 2 the sample period extends from 1919-T, and variables representing antitrust enforcement are included in the regression. This model takes the form

$$M_t = \alpha + \beta_1 X_{1_t} + \beta_2 X_{2_t} + \ldots + \beta_z X_{z_t} + \varphi AT_t + \sum_{r=1}^{q} \delta_r P_{r_t} \qquad (3\text{-}10)$$

where AT represents merger enforcement and $\sum_{r=1}^{q} P_r$ are dummy variables representing q precedent cases. More specifically, AT is defined as an index of weighted cumulative merger enforcement relative to merger activity. This variable represents the contribution to deterrence from enforcement (non-precedent) cases That is,

$$AT_t = \frac{\sum_{i=1}^{k} (w_i \cdot MC_{t-i})}{\sum_{i=1}^{k} (w_i \cdot M_{t-i})}$$

where w_i is the weighted value of the cumulative index of merger cases relative to merger activity during each of the preceding k years. The weighting scheme and number of years included in the index will be selected on the basis of the empirical results in the next chapter.

In equation 3-10 the coefficients of the dummy variables, $r = 1, \ldots$ q, represent the effect of precedent cases on the annual number of mergers. From this regression the number of mergers that would have occurred each year in the absence of Clayton 7 enforcement, M'_t, is predicted by

$$M'_t = M_t - \varphi \, AT_t - \sum_{r=1}^{q} \delta_r P_{r_t}$$

By subtracting actual merger activity from predicted merger activity, and dividing by the number of successful cases, average deterrence per case, $\overline{MD}$, can be estimated

$$\overline{MD} = \frac{\sum\limits_{t=1}^{T} (M'_t - M_t)}{\sum\limits_{t=1}^{T} MC_t}$$

The structure of the selected antitrust variables in equation 3-10 enables a distinction between deterrence resulting from precedent cases and deterrence from enforcement cases. Since

$$M'_t + \sum_{r=1}^{q} \delta_r P_{rt} = M_t - \varphi AT_t$$

the annual number of mergers that would have occurred in the absence of all enforcement case, M_{E_t}, is

$$M_{E_t} = M_t - \varphi AT_t$$

That is, the residual between observed merger activity in period t and the cumulative index of relative merger enforcement multiplied by its regression coefficient approximates merger activity if no enforcement cases had been undertaken. Subtracting actual merger activity from predicted merger activity yields a measure of average deterrence per enforcement case, $\overline{MD}_E$,

$$\overline{MD}_E = \frac{\sum\limits_{t=1}^{T} (M_{E_t} - M_t)}{\sum\limits_{t=1}^{T} MC_t}$$

Merger activity in the absence of any precedent case, s, can also be identified. Since

$$M'_t + \varphi\,AT_t + \sum_{\substack{r=0 \\ r \neq s}}^{q} \delta_r P_{r_t} = M_t - \delta_s P_{s_t}$$

the number of horizontal mergers that would have occurred had precedent case s not been undertaken is

$$M_{s_t} = M_t - \delta_s P_{s_t}$$

Thus, the amount of deterrence per year from case s is

$$MD_s = \frac{\sum_{t=1}^{T} (M_{s_t} - M_t)}{T}$$

If none of the precedent cases had occurred, the number of mergers that would have taken place, M_{P_t}, is measured by

$$M_{P_t} = M_t - \sum_{r=1}^{q} \delta_r P_{r_t}$$

and deterrence per year as a result of all the precedent cases is

$$MP_P = \frac{\sum_{t=1}^{T} (M_{P_t} - M_t)}{T}$$

Thus, equation 3-10 facilitates the estimation of merger activity if (1) there had been no horizontal merger enforcement; (2) there had been no enforcement cases, only precedent cases; and (3) there had been no precedent cases, only enforcement cases.

Although, on average, each case is attributed with preventing $\overline{MD}$ acquisitions from occurring, not all of the deterred mergers would have taken place in the same year that the case was filed. That is, if a case was undertaken in period i, it is unlikely that all of the deterred acquisitions would have also occurred in period i. There exists some structure of deterrence over periods i, i+1, . . . , i+k. Further, the deterrent effect may not be evenly distributed over the k periods following the case-filing date. It seems intuitive that deterrence is greater immediately after a case is filed than in more distant years.

One logical candidate for approximating the structure of deterrence is the number of years, and their respective weights, included in the cumulative index of relative merger enforcement in equation 3-10. If merger activity in period i is found to be affected by a case in period i−k, it follows that the deterrence will occur over the k periods following the case-filing date. Similarly, the relative influence on merger activity of the enforcement in the preceding years can be used to measure the proportion of deterrence occurring in each of the ensuing k years.

Using the value of shipments of the acquired firm in a case to approximate the size of each deterred merger, the deterrent effect, in dollar terms, DVS_a, is estimated by

$$DVS_a = \overline{MD} \cdot VS_a$$

Therefore, based on average deterrence, the indirect wealth redistribution benefit from a horizontal merger case, B_{qi}, is

$$B_{qi} = \sum_{n=1}^{N} \frac{\sum_{i=1}^{k} (w_i \cdot DVS_a) \cdot (1 - tr) \cdot b}{(1 + d)^n} \tag{3-10}$$

where $\sum_{i=1}^{k} w_i$ is the structure of deterrence in the years following a case that was previously discussed.

Summing the direct and indirect redistribution gains from a horizontal merger case yields the total benefit (B_q),

$$B_q = B_{qd} + B_{qi}$$

Allocative Efficiency

Direct Effect

A horizontal merger case also provides an improvement in allocative efficiency. The direct gain is the deadweight loss avoided by prohibiting the merger. As discussed previously, a merger increasing the four-firm concentration ratio has the effect of changing the price-cost margin, represented in figure 3-2 from (p_1 cfd) to (p_2 cea). Such an increase in the price-

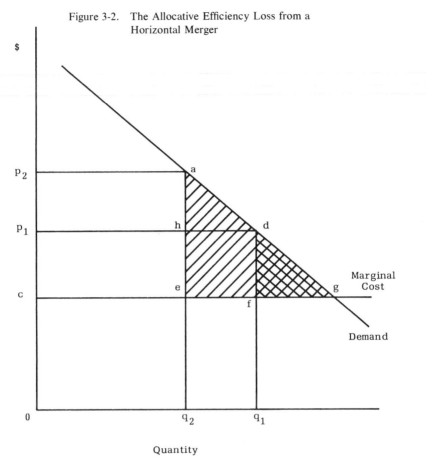

Figure 3-2.   The Allocative Efficiency Loss from a Horizontal Merger

cost margin leads to a reduction in allocative efficiency, W, which is measured by [16]

$$W = 1/2 \, (p_2 - p_1) \cdot (q_2 - q_1)$$

Since

$$(q_2 - q_1) = \frac{(q_2 - q_1)/q_2}{(p_2 - p_1)/p_2} \cdot \frac{(p_2 - p_1)}{P_2} \cdot q_2$$

it follows that

$$W = 1/2 \, (p_2 - p_1) \cdot \frac{(p_2 - p_1)}{p_2} \cdot q_2 \cdot \eta$$

$$= 1/2 \frac{(p_2 - p_1)^2}{p_2} \cdot q_2 \cdot \eta$$

where

$$\eta = \frac{(q_2 - q_1)/q_1}{(p_2 - p_1)/p_2}$$

The industry value of shipments, VS, represents $(p_2 \cdot q_2)$, and $(p_2 - p_1)/p_2$ can be approximated as a price-cost markup by $\{((VS + VS_a) - (CM + W))/(VS + VS_a)\} - \{(VS - (CM + W))/VS\}$. Therefore

$$W = 1/2 \left(\frac{VS + VS_a - (CM + W)}{VS + VS_a} - \frac{VS - (CM + W)}{VS} \right) \cdot VS \cdot \eta$$

The change in the price-cost margin is linearly related to the change in the four-firm concentration ratio, as discussed previously. As a result of the merger

$$\frac{VS + VS_a - (CM + W)}{VS + VS_a} - \frac{VS - (CM + W)}{VS} = b \cdot \Delta\, CR$$

Since

$$b \cdot \Delta\, CR = b \cdot \frac{VS_a}{VS}$$

the allocative gain from a successful merger case is

$$W = 1/2 \left(b \cdot \frac{VS_a}{VS} \right)^2 \cdot VS \cdot \eta = 1/2\, b^2 \cdot \frac{VS_a}{VS} \cdot VS_a \cdot \eta$$

The net direct benefit from the gain in allocative efficiency, B_{fd}, is

$$B_{fd} = \sum_{n=0}^{N} \frac{1/2\, b^2\, (VS_a/VS) \cdot VS_a \cdot \eta \cdot V_n}{(1 + d)^n} \tag{3-11}$$

where V_n is assigned a value of zero in the years prior to obtaining effective relief and a value of one in all following years. That is, $V_n = 0$ if $n^* > n$, and $V_n = 1$ if $n^* \leq n$, where n^* is the period when divestiture is achieved.

Indirect Effect

Mergers deterred by a case also represent an indirect gain in allocative efficiency. The number of mergers that would have occurred in the absence of a horizontal merger case is estimated by the two methods discussed in previous sections. Using the average deterrence measure, $\overline{MD}$, to estimate the indirect effect, B_{fi}, and substituting into equation 3-11 yields

$$B_{fi} = \sum_{n=1}^{N} 1/2 \, b^2 \, \frac{\sum_{i=1}^{k} \left((w_i \cdot \overline{MD}) \cdot (VS_a)^2 / VS \cdot \eta \right)}{(1 + d)^n} \tag{3-12}$$

Hence, the total allocative efficiency benefit from a horizontal merger case is

$$B_f = B_{fd} + B_{fi}$$

In chapter 4 the two methods of estimating the deterrent effect will be used to obtain different measures of deterrence. In chapter 6, based on the derived measures of the redistribution benefits and allocative efficiency benefits, the gain from deterrence will be added to the direct benefits, and then compared with the cost of undertaking a merger case, enabling an evaluation of horizontal merger enforcement.

4

The Celler-Kefauver Act and the Deterrent Effect

Introduction

This chapter attempts to address the counter-factual question: "How many horizontal mergers causing increases in the industry four-firm concentration ratio would have occurred in the absence of the Celler-Kefauver Act and its subsequent enforcement?" The answer to this question provides a measure of deterrence—the number of mergers that were not undertaken as a result of antitrust activity. The focus of this chapter is the estimation of models explaining merger activity so that inferences can be drawn about the magnitude of the effect of the Celler-Kefauver Act.

This excusion into the counter-factual is essential in a cost-benefit study of the Celler-Kefauver Act since the deterrent effect it provides is a major source of benefits. In fact, Jesse Markham wrote that deterrence is *the* major benefit: ". . . it is relevant to inquire into the effect Section 7 has had on the volume of mergers it presumably was designed to prohibit. In any society governed by law it is generally expected that the law's principal effect is to be found in its observance rather than its breach."[1]

The need for measuring the deterrent effect has been recognized previously by antitrust researchers: "The beneficial results from antitrust activities have come from neither the number of firms forced to divest, nor the number of mergers prevented from being consummated, but can only be found in the deterrent presented to the very largest firms, those perhaps overly cautious because of their high visibility. Even though antitrust policy has not been successful, it would take an excursion into counter-factual history to determine more precisely what that level might have been, a task better left to the more intrepid of the 'new economic historians.' "[2]

Despite this recognition, no such measurement of the deterrent effect has been undertaken, perhaps for the reason given by Richard J. Arnould: "It remains difficult to determine the appropriate manner in which to estimate the duration of the effect, particularly in the case of mergers, and even more perplexing, the deterrent effect."[3]

Given the pitfalls of measuring and comparing a counter-factual world to the actual historical experience, extreme care must be used in methodology. In this chapter two distinct methods are employed to estimate the deterrent effect. The first method estimates a model explaining horizontal mergers increasing the four-firm concentration ratio over a pre-Celler-Kefauver enforcement period. The number of such mergers that would have occurred in the absence of antitrust enforcement during successive years is predicted by extrapolating from the historical values of the explanatory variables. The residual between predicted merger activity and actual merger activity is then attributed to deterrence.

There are two major assumptions implicit in this method of extrapolation. First, the validity of such an extrapolation depends upon the assumption that the relationship between the explanatory variables and merger activity is invariant over time. To the degree that the structure of the model is unstable with respect to time, predicted merger activity will not yield an accurate estimate. Second, this method assumes that deterrence accounts for the entire difference between predicted and actual merger activity. Any effect, positive or negative, that events external to the model have on merger activity, such as the political environment or changes in tax law, are attributed to deterrence. That is, other variables may account for some of the residual between predicted and actual merger activity, but the entire residual is assumed to be the result of antitrust enforcement.

Because of the tenuous nature of these assumptions, a second procedure is also used to measure deterrence. Rather than estimating deterrence indirectly as a residual, this method includes variables representing antitrust enforcement in a model estimating merger activity. Merger activity in the absence of antitrust is predicted by subtracting these variables multiplied by their respective regression coefficients from the observed number of mergers. Deterrence is then measured by the difference between actual merger activity and predicted merger activity. The advantage of this method is that deterrence is measured directly by the antitrust variables in the model; this allows for a separation between the influence of antitrust activity and pure "noise" and therefore a more exact identification of the effect on merger activity from antitrust.

The major weakness of this method is the lack of any theoretical basis for the specification of antitrust enforcement variables. There is no a priori knowledge of a specific structural form from which to model the effect of antitrust enforcement on merger activity. No defense of any particular model can be made that would foreclose all other models. Therefore, several different representations of antitrust enforcement are used and compared.

Because of the strengths and weaknesses of each procedure for measuring deterrence, both types of models are estimated. This allows for a lower-limit and an upper-limit measure of deterrence. Since this chapter is an expedition into the counter-factual, such bounds probably yield more information than a single estimate.

Data

The models to be presented and empirically tested predict horizontal merger activity based on the level of antitrust enforcement and other variables. If previous researchers of merger activity had this study in mind, perhaps a series would now exist listing all of the horizontal mergers increasing the four-firm concentration ratio that occurred between the early 1900s and the present. Naturally, such a list would include the size of both the acquiring and acquired firms, in terms of value of shipments, as well as the value of the firm's shipments in each market. A generous list might even identify each firm's market share relative to the entire market for every product the firm sells.

Unfortunately, no such list exists. There are no previously-identified series of horizontal mergers increasing the four-firm concentration ratio. However, there are several overlapping series, beginning in the late 1800s, identifying all the firms that acquired another firm, were acquired by another firm, or a member of a consolidation. Therefore (using the procedure to be discussed), it was possible to construct an index of large horizontal merger activity by splicing the existing series together.

There are three major historical series of recorded mergers that, when combined, span the twentieth century to date: (1) Ralph L. Nelson,[4] 1895 to 1920; (2) Carl Eis,[5] 1919 to 1930; and (3) Federal Trade Commission[6] (incorporating a 1919-39 series by Willard Thorp[7]), 1919 to the present. To avoid splicing all three series together, yet still including the second merger wave which occurred during the late 1920s, the period from 1919 to 1976 was selected. Therefore, the horizontal merger series used in this book is based on the Eis series and the FTC series.

There are three major reasons for not including the earlier merger series. First, as previously stated, this avoids the problems of data compatibility confronted when combining different series based on slightly different criteria. Second, it is a heroic assumption to expect a stable relationship between horizontal merger activity and the explanatory variables over a fifty-eight year period. It is even more heroic to extend this assumption to a larger time period. Third, Nelson's data do not always indicate the type of merger, nor is the four-digit industry always identified. There is not enough information in the worksheets Nelson compiled, nor are there sufficient ancillary sources of information available for the relevant time period listing the industries each firm sells in, as well as its share of the total sales in each market, to incorporate the data into the series used in this work, without making extreme assumptions. For these three reasons, 1919 was selected as the first observation.

Both the "Basic Worksheets" used by Eis and the FTC series are essentially lists identifying firms involved in all large acquisitions and consolidations occurring in a given year. Both the Eis series and the FTC series include only mergers and acquisitions in manufacturing and mining industries. The scope of this work is therefore limited to the manufacturing sector.

Carl Eis recorded 3,009 acquisitions and consolidations between 1919-30. His main source was the *Commercial and Financial Chronicle*. An acquisition or consolidation was included in the merger series if it represented the disappearance of a separate decision-making entity, engaged in manufacturing or mining. Eis reports there is a tendency for mergers involving small firms to be ignored by the *Chronicle*. Therefore, his sample may exclude some of the merger activity among companies with few assets.

Fortunately, Eis's worksheets, which are the basis for the aggregated total number of mergers annually, identify the type of merger, the relevant four-digit or three-digit industry, and frequently some measure of size of the merger. Assuming Eis's data to be as accurate as is realistically possible, his categorization of merger type—horizontal, vertical, or diversification—was used to pre-sort the data between horizontal mergers and non-horizontal mergers.

A selection criterion was used to identify the "large" mergers— mergers increasing the four-firm concentration ratio. If Eis commented on his worksheet that the acquiring or acquired firm was among the largest four firms in the industry, the merger was included in the large horizontal merger series used in this paper. If Eis gave no information about the relative market size of the firm, the *Statistical Report: Value of Shipments Data By Product Class for the 1,000 Largest Manufacturing Companies of 1950*[8] was used to identify the combined firms' share of the value of shipments in the industry affected by the horizontal merger; if the consolidated firm was one of the largest four firms in the industry in 1950 the merger was included in the large horizontal merger series. This identification procedure assumes that since the firm was sufficiently large relative to other firms in the industry in 1950, the firm was most likely among the largest four in the year the merger is registered in Eis's data. Such an assumption is not likely to be incorrect in very many cases for this time period. It should be remembered that few mergers occurred in the years 1930 to 1950 and that more than half of the mergers recorded by Eis took place after 1925.

Not all of the firms on Eis's "Worksheets" appear in the 1950 *Statistical Report*. These firms may have been acquired by another firm during the interim or just too small to be among the largest 1,000 firms in the country in 1950. In this situation, the assets of each of the largst firms in the industry were compared using Moody's, and if the merged firm appeared to be among the four largest firms in the industry at the time of the merger it was included in the large horizontal merger series.

Based on the selection criterion, the large horizontal merger series— the number of horizontal mergers in manufacturing increasing the four-firm concentration ration—was formed.

Although the Federal Trade Commission publishes the aggregate number of mergers annually between 1919 to the present, information identifying the individual firms merging during the period 1919 to 1946 is unavailable (the underlying "worksheets" containing this information have disappeared). The FTC does identify all large mergers in manufacturing from 1948 to 1976 along with the type of merger, four- or three-digit SIC industry, asset sizes of acquiring and acquired firms, among other characteristics.[9]

For the period 1948 to 1961, whether the merger increased the four-firm concentration ratio was determined by comparing the combined firms' value of shipments with those of the largest firms in the relevant industry identified by the 1950 *Statistical Report*.[10] For the period 1962 to 1976, this same procedure was used except that the firm and industry data published by the EIS (Economic Information Service) was substituted. Implementing this selection criterion from the FTC merger series was the basis for the large horizontal merger series, 1948-76.

Unfortunately, no information identifying merging firms by name and industry similar to the 1948-76 FTC data and Eis's 1919-30 data exists for the period 1931 to 1947. There is, however, information on the number of mergers each year published by the FTC. Although these data do not segregate the various types of mergers, nor list the individual firms involved, they do provide vital information enabling an estimate of the annual number of large horizontal mergers over this period. The problem presented by these missing observations can be remedied using the aggregate number of mergers published by the FTC in a procedure recommended by G. S. Maddala.[11] In situations where data are unavailable, Maddala suggests approximating the missing data by a "zero-order regression method." Each missing value is substituted by the mean of the known values. If observations of samples n_1 and n_3 are known for a variable x, the value of x for the sample n_2 can be approximated by assigning a value of x—the mean value of x from $n_1 + n_3$ observations—to each of the missing observations in n_2.

This method was modified somewhat to accommodate the information available from the FTC data. As stated previously, the total number of mergers from 1919 to 1930 and 1948 to 1976 can be obtained from existing sources. A first approximation might be to compute the ratio of large horizontal acquisitions to total mergers using the known observations, and assume that an identical ratio exists for the period with unknown observations for the number of large horizontal mergers. Since total merger activity is known during the 1931-47 period, the number of large horizontal mergers could then be interpolated.

However, the proportion of large horizontal mergers relative to total merger activity varies considerably between the 1919-30 and post-1947 periods. Hence, a method was employed to adjust for this variation between periods. There were 413 large horizontal mergers and a total of 8,055 acquisitions of all types and sizes recorded between 1919 and 1930. The ratio of large horizontal mergers to the total number of mergers is .051. Since the first successful post-Celler-Kefauver case was initiated in 1954, 1953 was used as a cut-off date for the post-1947 period. Between 1948 and 1953 the proportion of large horizontal mergers to the total number of acquisitions was .01.

The ratio of large horizontal mergers to total mergers was assumed to decline by a constant amount each year, from .051 in 1930, the year prior to the interpolation period, to .01 in 1948, the year following the period of interpolation. Therefore, in each year during the interpolation period, the ratio declined by a constant amount, .0024, from the previous year. Algebraically, the ratio of large horizontal mergers to total mergers over the 1931-47 period is assumed to be a constant declining linear combination of the form:

$$\left(\frac{L}{M}\right)_t = \left(\frac{L}{M}\right)_{t-1} - \left(\frac{\sum\limits_{1919}^{1930} L}{\sum\limits_{1919}^{1930} M} + \frac{\sum\limits_{1948}^{1953} L}{\sum\limits_{1948}^{1953} M}\right) \bigg/ 2 = \left(\frac{L}{M}\right)_{t-1} - .0024$$

where L is the number of large horizontal mergers, M is the total number of mergers in the FTC series, and $(L/M)_{t-1}$ is set equal to .051 in the initial period of interpolation, t=1931, and t ranges from 1931-47. In the final period of interpolation, t=1947, $(L/M)_{t-1}$ = .01.

Since the total number of mergers is known over this period, the number of large horizontal mergers is estimated using these interpolated ratios. This procedure is based on the known values of large horizontal merger activity, total merger activity, and their relative trends over time. Evidence can be inferred from the empirical analysis discussed later in the chapter that these data seem reasonable; deleting the 1931-47 time period from the analysis does not greatly alter the results. Further, because of the very low level of total merger activity during this period, different ratios do not produce a great divergence from the number of large horizontal mergers estimated by the preceding procedure.

The other major data used in this chapter is the number of horizontal merger cases undertaken annually. The main source used to identify all Celler-Kefauver enforcement is *The Celler-Kefauver Act: The First 27 Years*,[12] a study prepared by Professor Willard F. Mueller for the use of the Judiciary Committee of Congress. This source lists all of the 272 merger cases undertaken by the Justice Department and all of the 164 merger cases undertaken by the FTC. The date of complaint, challenged company, acquired company, relevant markets, and information about industry and company characteristics are stated in this source. To gain additional information about the type of merger and the companies involved, the *Merger Case Digest*[13] reveals more specific details and also categorizes the merger case as "horizontal," "vertical," or "conglomerate." This enables an accurate assessment of the type of merger involved in each case.

Many mergers involved more than one aspect, such as both horizontal and vertical, or both horizontal and conglomerate, or all three. In these situations, the merger was included in the list of horizontal merger cases used in this work, since the horizontal aspects of the case would be expected to contribute to deterrence. Only in the few cases that the *Merger Case Digest* indicated had trivial horizontal aspects was this classification not followed.

Because the merger series is limited in scope to the manufacturing sector, the inclusion of merger cases to the merger case indexes used in this study was also constrainted to manufacturing industries to maintain consistency. Retail trade, the financial sector, newspapers, mining, and transportation are all excluded. However, merger cases of all sizes were included in the merger case indexes even though the merger series includes only those mergers increasing an industry's four-firm concentration ratio. Merger cases involving small firms certainly provide a deterrent effect. In fact, the deterrence from these cases may actually exceed the deterrent effect from a case involving larger firms: If smaller firms are being prosecuted, the perceived probability of larger firms merging and remaining unscathed by the antitrust authorities may diminish.

There does not have to be a successful court decision (from the enforcement perspective) for the case to be included in the merger case index; there must, however, be a successful outcome. If the case is dropped because the firm agrees to a mutually-agreed-upon divestiture in an out-of-court settlement or a consent decree is entered, the case is considered successful.

Of the merger cases initiated by the antitrust agencies, 289 were brought against firms engaged in manufacturing and mining. Fifty-seven per cent, or 163, of these cases were manufacturing firms making horizontal acquisitions. Twenty of the cases were either lost by the antitrust agencies or dropped without obtaining at least partial divestiture. Thus, 143 of the horizontal merger cases in manufacturing were successful. Of the 436 merger cases initiated by the antitrust agencies, 143 met the described selection criteria.

Models Explaining Merger Activity

As discussed in chapter 2, previous studies have identified variables indicating general economic activity as being correlated with merger activity. Factors typically associated with the business cycle, Standard and Poor's Stock Price Index,[14] and the prime interest rate[15] were considered for explanatory variables in the regression models used in this chapter.

The first type of model attempts to explain merger activity prior to effective enforcement of the Celler-Kefauver Act. This method assumes that the structure of the estimated model would have remained intact during the subsequent years had there been no Celler-Kefauver Act and no antitrust litigation. Therefore, the year selected as representing the commencement of effective horizontal merger enforcement is critical—this critical year indicates the end of a year with virtually only Sherman Act constraints on merger activity, and the beginning of an era prohibiting potentially anti-competitive mergers.

There are three likely candidates for the critical year representing the change from ineffective to effective horizontal merger enforcement: (1) 1955, the year following the first successful merger case, was also the year that the Antitrust Division first engaged in Celler-Kefauver enforcement by undertaking five cases; this signified the willingness and determination of the antitrust agencies to undertake merger cases; (2) 1962, after the major precedent-setting case, *Brown Shoe*, which clarified the Supreme Court's interpretation of the Celler-Kefauver Act; and (3) 1950, the year Congress amended the original Section 7 of the Clayton Act by passing the Celler-Kefauver Act. Models using each of these candidates as the critical years were estimated, enabling deterrence to be measured using the procedures discussed in chapter 2.

Using 1955 as the critical year representing a switch in regimes from the ineffective to effective horizontal merger enforcement, the following model of merger activity was estimated (standard error in parentheses)

$$M = -12.40 + .83SP + 6.64PR \qquad (4\text{-}1)$$
$$ (8.39) \quad (.51) \quad (1.37)^*$$

$$\overline{R}^2 = .42 \qquad F = 12.07^* \qquad RSS = 7697.49$$

where M is the number of large horizontal mergers attempted, SP is Standard and Poor's Stock Price Index, and PR is the prime interest rate. M includes not only the large horizontal mergers occurring, but also those proposed but never consummated or divested because of an antitrust case. This measure of merger activity is referred to in *The Celler-Kefauver Act: The First 27 Years,* as "actual and proposed large acquisitions."

Thus, M measures not only the publicly reported mergers but also large horizontal mergers listed in FTC and Justice Department complaints not appearing in the large merger series. The number of mergers predicted by this equation in the years following 1954 is given by assigning the observed values of SP_t and PR_t into equation 4-1.

For example, in 1955 the stock price index was 42.40 and the prime interest rate was 1.58 percent. Inserting these values into equation 4-1 yields a predicted value of merger activity equal to 33.28. Deterrence in 1955 is then measured as the difference between predicted merger activity, M_t', and observed merger activity, or $M_t' - M_t$. Since there were 21 large horizontal mergers actually attempted in 1955, deterrence is estimated by

$$12.28 = M_t' - M_t$$

where t = 1955.

Repeating this procedure for each year measures the total amount of deterrence resulting from the Celler-Kefauver Act and its subsequent enforcement. Over the twenty-two year period following 1954 an average of 80.82 mergers were deterred annually. On average, each of the 143 cases contributed 12.43 mergers to the deterrent effect. This is referred to as

*Used throughout this book to connote "Significant at 95% level of confidence."

"average deterrence"—the amount of deterrence per case—in chapter 3.

A regression similar to (4-1) was run, but the period was extended to 1919-61. This assumed that the *Brown Shoe* decision marked the change from ineffective to effective horizontal merger enforcement. Because this major precedent case clearly enunciating the Supreme Court's interpretation of the Celler-Kefauver Amendment did not occur until 1962, a dummy variable was added to the basic model to distinguish between the years before and after effective enforcement of the Celler-Kefauver Act. In the following equation

$$M = -1.18 + .28SP + 5.58PR - 16.78CK \qquad (4\text{-}2)$$
$$(4.79)\ \ (.24)\quad (1.22)^*\quad (8.77)$$

$$\overline{R}^2 = .39 \qquad F = 8.68^* \qquad RSS = 8542.15$$

CK is assigned the value of zero prior to 1962 and the value of one for 1962 and all following years. The difference between predicted and actual merger activity, $M_t' - M_t$, is 500.87 for 1962 to 1976. This represents 33.39 mergers per year that would have occurred in the absence of antitrust enforcement. The 86 cases after 1961 had an average of 5.82 mergers deterred.

These measures of deterrence from equation 4-2 actually understate the effect of antitrust enforcement on merger activity. Because the Celler-Kefauver dummy variable represents 16.78 mergers that would have occurred annually without the Act's passage, the total number of large horizontal mergers deterred since 1950 is 1953.27, or an average of 35.31 mergers per year over this period. Average deterrence is then estimated as 6.69 mergers per horizontal merger case.

Although CK is not statistically significant at the 95% confidence level, equation 4-2 implicitly attributes 16.78 mergers deterred per year to the Celler-Kefauver Act. This suggests that 1950 may be the appropriate critical year depicting the transition in regimes of different legal environments for horizontal mergers. Using 1950 as the critical year, and estimating the model for the period 1919 to 1949, produced:

$$M = -32.67 + 2.66SP + 7.38PR \qquad (4\text{-}3)$$
$$(-8.56)^*\ \ (.61)^*\quad (1.16)^*$$

$$\overline{R}^2 = .62 \qquad F = 23.84^* \qquad RSS = 4732.53$$

The explanatory power of equation 4-3 is considerably more powerful than either of its predecessors. Similarly, in equation 4-3, both the stock price index and the prime rate have a statistically significant effect on merger activity; only the prime rate is significant in equations 4-1 and 4-2.

Because the coefficients of both explanatory variables are larger in value in equation 4-3 than in the two prior regressions, predicted merger activity, and therefore deterrence, is much larger. From 1950 to 1976, average deterrence per case is 35.01; 185.43 mergers are deterred annually.

Of these three equations, which is the regression representing the true pre-effective merger enforcement regime? The signs of the coefficients in each of the regressions are consistent. The values of these coefficients, though different for each regression, do not differ radically. However, because predicted merger activity, and therefore deterrence, is very sensitive to the magnitude of the regression coefficients, each model estimates a slightly different amount of deterrence. These differences can be attributed to the information contained in the regressions included in years after 1950. That is, although equations 4-1 and 4-2 may represent the critical years separating ineffective and effective merger enforcement, estimating a model up to 1954 or 1961 still contains some effect from the Celler-Kefauver Act. This effect, if strong enough, may tend to bias the explanatory variables and obscure the "true" effect of these variables on the dependent variable. Essentially, in these regressions there may be explanatory variables—presumably representing antitrust enforcement—missing from the equation.

On the other hand, the regression using 1950 as the critical year may be including non-antitrust effects in the measures of deterrence. If the true relationship between stock price index, prime interest rate, and merger activity is different during the 1950s and 1960s than in earlier years, imposing a pre-1950 model on subsequent years to measure deterrence is less accurate than regressions with 1955 and 1962 as critical years. The regressions that include more information are more likely to yield reliable results. The later the critical year and estimation period, the more information is included in the coefficient estimates, and the more likely it is that the estimated coefficients of the explanatory variables will be accurate for the period of extrapolation.

The dilemma of assessing the appropriate critical year is that the 1919-49 regression is not subject to omitted antitrust variables, but may be excluding information on the post-war relationship between the explanatory variables and the dependent variable; the 1919-61 regression includes more information on the post-war relationship between the explanatory variables and the dependent variable, but may have biased coefficients due to omitted antitrust variables. This dilemma is somewhat resolved in the last section of this chapter using information from the models estimated by the alternative method of explaining merger activity.

Method 2

The second method for estimating deterrence avoids the problems of assuming that the estimated coefficients are stable over the estimated and extrapolated periods. By including variables representing antitrust enforcement, the effect of antitrust on merger activity can be estimated directly. Deterrence is measured by the difference between predicted merger activity, with the antitrust variables assigned a value of zero, and observed merger activity. As discussed in chapter 3, there are two determinants of the deterrent effect from a case—the value from setting a precedent and the value from enforcing an existing precedent. The precedent value of a case is represented by a dummy variable which is assigned a value of zero prior to the year of the Supreme Court's decision, and a value of one for all subsequent years. Three dummy variables are included in the models to represent institutional changes in the legal environment; these represent (1) passage of the Celler-Kefauver Act in 1950, (2) *Brown Shoe* in 1962, and (3) *Von's Grocery* in 1966.

The second determinant of deterrence is the effect from enforcing an existing precedent. The greater enforcement is relative to the number of mergers, the lower will be the perceived probability by firms of evading the antitrust agencies and completing the merger. This is represented by an index of relative merger enforcement—the number of horizontal merger cases during a given period divided by the number of large horizontal mergers attempted for that same period. A cumulative index of relative merger enforcement that includes information from previous recent years is probably a more appropriate measure of antitrust enforcement than the relative merger enforcement of only each year. It is unlikely that firms in 1968 based their decision to merge only on the relative merger enforcement of the previous year; if there were only a few cases in 1967, but many cases in 1966, firms most likely would still perceive a vigorous enforcement effort.

Firms probably are acutely sensitive to the relative merger enforcement during the preceding years. However, there is no a priori theory answering the questions, "How many years?" and "How sensitive?"Therefore, the empirical evidence was used as the guideline to answer these questions. After testing with cumulative indexes it was found that including information from either the previous four or six years in the index yielded the best results on the basis of t-tests. This answered the question of how many previous years relative enforcement affected the current year's merger activity. The question of how sensitive the current year's merger activity is to the previous years' relative merger activity is answered by assigning weights to each year's index. Presumably the most recent year is weighted most heavily and the most distant year is weighted least heavily. Different weighting schemes are reported with different models, depending upon the lags included in the cumulative index.

Using a cumulative relative merger index including the previous four years, merger activity was estimated as

$$M = -.288 + .54SP + 5.10PR - 23.47AT_1 - 18.41CK \qquad (4\text{-}4)$$
$$(-4.63)(.24)^* \quad (1.01)^* \quad (-15.07) \quad (-6.98)^*$$

$$-11.33B - 24.13V$$
$$(-10.88)(-9.96)^*$$

$$\overline{R}^2 = .39 \qquad F = 5.67^* \qquad RSS = 8542.15$$

where CK is a dummy variable representing passage of the Celler-Kefauver Act, B is a dummy variable representing the Supreme Court's *Brown Shoe* decision, V is a dummy variable representing the Supreme Court's *Von's Grocery* decision, and AT_1 is a lagged four-year cumulative index of relative merger enforcement, where

$$AT_{1t} = MC4_{t-1} / MA4_{t-1}$$

and

$$MC4_t = MC_t + \sum_{j=1}^{3} (MC_{t-j} \times .5^j)$$
$$MA4_t = M_t + \sum_{j=1}^{3} (M_{t-j} \times .5^j)$$

and MC_t is the number of selected horizontal merger cases occurring in period t.

Of the antitrust variables, only the Celler-Kefauver and *Von's Grocery* dummy variables have a significant effect on merger activity. All of the antitrust variables' coefficients have the expected negative sign. The Durbin-Watson statistic is not reported because lagged values of the dependent variable are in the denominator of AT_1. This means that the error term is not independent of the dependent variable; therefore, the D-W statistic has no meaning.[16]

Equation 4-2 provides information about the effect of antitrust enforcement on merger activity. Using standard F-tests, three questions about the effectiveness of merger enforcement can be answered: (1) Do the precedent cases contribute significantly to deterring merger activity?

(2) Do the non-precedent cases contribute significantly to deterring merger activity? and (3) Does the total enforcement of the Celler-Kefauver Act significantly deter merger activity? By restricting the coefficients of CK, B, and V to equal zero, $\beta_{CK} = \beta_B = \beta_V = 0$, and comparing the restricted and unrestricted sum of squared residuals, the first question can be answered. By restricting the coefficient of AT_1 to equal zero, $\beta_{AT} = 0$, and comparing the restricted and unrestricted sum of squared residuals, the second question can be answered. Finally, by setting the coefficients of all the antitrust variables equal to zero, $\beta_{CK} = \beta_B = \beta_V = \beta_{AT} = 0$, and comparing the restricted and unrestricted sum of squared residuals, the third question can be answered.

The results are shown in table 4-1. All of the F-statistics are significant at the 95% confidence level. This suggests that both the precedent and non-precedent cases contribute significantly to deterrence, and that the entire horizontal merger enforcement bundle has significantly influenced merger activity.

Table 4-1.   F-Tests for the Significance of Merger Enforcement from Equation 4-4

Restriction	Restricted Sum of Squared Residuals	Unrestricted Sum of Squared Residuals	F
$\beta_{CK} = \beta_B = \beta_V = 0$	10410.30	8542.15	3.72*
$\beta_{AT_1} = 0$	8948.70	8542.15	2.43*
$\beta_{CK} = \beta_B = \beta_V = \beta_{AT_1} = 0$	10493.30	8542.15	2.43*

Equation 4-4 enables some differentiation between the assessment of the precedent and enforcement value from antitrust. As described in chapter 3, merger activity in the absence of precedent enforcement can be predicted by

$$M_E' = M - (\beta_{AT_1} \times AT_1)$$

Deterrence resulting from enforcement cases which did not set precedents is measured by

$$MD_E = M_E' - M$$

Using the estimated coefficients in equation 4-4, and summing over the period 1950 to 1976, $MD_E = 350.27$, or 2.63 mergers deterred per case.

Merger activity in the absence of the precedent cases, including the passage of the Celler-Kefauver Act, can be predicted by

$$M_P' = M - (\beta_{CK} \times CK) - (\beta_B \times B) - (\beta_V \times V)$$

Deterrence resulting from the precedent cases and passage of the Celler-Kefauver Act is measured by

$$MD_P = M_P' - M$$

Using the estimated coefficients in equation 4-4, and summing over the period 1950 to 1976, $MD_P = 932.37$. Thus, precedent value accounts for an average of 34.53 mergers deterred per year. Interestingly, the Celler-Kefauver dummy accounts for 18.41 mergers deterred annually; this is very close to the 16.78 mergers deterred annually attributed to the Celler-Kefauver legislation in equation 4-2.

Total deterrence, MD, is the sum of deterrence from relative enforcement and deterrence from precedent cases:

$$MD = MD_E + MD_P$$

Over the twenty-seven year period, an average of 47.51 mergers were deterred annually; average deterrence is 8.98 mergers per case.

A similar model was estimated, but the cumulative index of relative merger enforcement was extended to include the previous six, instead of four, years' information. Because of the smaller influence of previous years, less weight was placed on the most distant years included in the index. That is,

$$AT_2 = MC6_{t-1} / MA6_{t-1}$$

where

$$MC6 = MC_t + \sum_{j=1}^{5} (MC_{t-j} \times .7^j)$$
$$MA6 = M_t + \sum_{j=1}^{5} (M_{t-j} \times .7^j)$$

This model produced somewhat more satisfactory results: (4-5)

$$M = -4.73 \quad + .66SP \quad + 5.27PR \quad - 41.34AT_2$$
$$(-4.82) \quad (.26)^* \quad (1.04)^* \quad (-20.53)^*$$

$$- 18.36CK \quad - 14.31B \quad - 24.17V$$
$$(-6.91)^* \quad (-10.13) \quad (-9.59)^*$$

$$\overline{R}^2 = .40 \qquad F = 5.79^* \qquad RSS = 8277.72$$

All of the antitrust variables are statistically significant with the exception of the *Brown Shoe* dummy variable. Unlike the preceding model, the relative merger index is significant in equation 4-5. The values of the coefficients of AT_1 and AT_2 are not comparable because these indexes differ in their numerical values. However, the coefficients of both the control explanatory variables—SP and PR—and the precedent dummy variables, especially CK and V, are almost identical between equations 4-4 and 4-5. This suggests that the estimation is not particularly sensitive to the length of lags included in the cumulative index of relative merger enforcement; a comforting result, since these lags were arbitrarily selected.

Placing restrictions on the antitrust coefficients allows for F-tests on the significance of merger enforcement. As shown in table 4-2 both the precedent cases and non-precedent cases, as well as the entire bundle of merger enforcement, significantly affected merger activity.

Table 4-2.   F-Tests for the Significance of Merger Enforcement from
Equation 4-5

Restriction	Restricted Sum of Squared Residuals	Unrestricted Sum of Squared Residuals	F
$\beta_{CK} = \beta_B = \beta_V = 0$	10142.90	8277.72	3.83*
$\beta_{AT_1} = 0$	8948.70	8277.72	4.70*
$\beta_{CK} = \beta_B = \beta_V = \beta_{AT_1} = 0$	10493.30	8277.72	3.41*

The enforcement cases deterred 582.07 mergers, or 4.07 mergers per case. The precedent cases deterred 906.99 mergers, or 33.59 mergers per year. Total deterrence is therefore 1489.06; average deterrence is 10.42 mergers per case.

There does not appear to be any major difference between models using four and six year lags in the cumulative index of relative merger-enforcement. Deterrence differs by only 7.64 mergers per year or 1.44 mergers per case. Similarly, the deterrence attributed to the precedent cases is remarkably consistent between the models—the deterrence per year from precedent cases in equation 4-5 exceeds the equivalent measure in equation 4-4 by only .94 mergers per year, or a total of 25.38 mergers over the entire period.

Models similar to equations 4-4 and 4-5 but using an unweighted cumulative index of relative merger enforcement were estimated. In these models

$$AT_3 = MC4_{t-1} / MA4_{t-1}$$

where

$$MC4 = \sum_{j=0}^{3} MC_{t-j}$$

$$MA4 = \sum_{j=0}^{3} M_{t-j}$$

and

$$AT_4 = MC6_{t-1} / MA6_{t-1}$$

where

$$MC6 = \sum_{j=0}^{5} MC_{t-j}$$

$$MA6 = \sum_{j=0}^{5} M_{t-j}$$

Including the previous four years in the unweighted merger enforcement index produced

$$
\begin{aligned}
M = -\,&7.09 \quad\;\; + .85SP \quad + 5.37PR \quad - 59.43AT_3 \\
&(-5.00) \quad (.29)^* \qquad (.99)^* \qquad (-24.00)^* \qquad\qquad (4\text{-}6)\\
-\,&20.67CK \;-\; 25.43V \;-\; 14.46B \\
&(-6.86)^* \quad (-9.33)^* \quad (-9.80)
\end{aligned}
$$

$$\bar{R}^2 = .42 \qquad F = 5.39^* \qquad RSS = 7989.85$$

With the exception of the *Brown Shoe* dummy variable, all of the estimated coefficients are significant at the 95% confidence level. Unlike the weighted version of this model, the cumulative index of relative merger enforcement has a statistically significant affect on merger activity. The Celler-Kefauver and *Von's* dummy variables have slightly larger coefficients and the *Brown Shoe* dummy variable has a slightly smaller coefficient in the unweighted than in the weighted version. As shown in table 4-3, placing restrictions on the antitrust coefficients and performing the relevant F-tests shows that the precedent cases, the enforcement cases, and the entire bundle of merger enforcement significantly affect merger activity.

Table 4-3.   F-Tests for the Significance of Merger Enforcement from Equation 4-6

Restriction	Restricted Sum of Squared Residuals	Unrestricted Sum of Squared Residuals	F
$\beta_{CK} = \beta_B = \beta_V = 0$	10067.00	7989.45	4.41*
$\beta_{AT_1} = 0$	8948.70	7989.45	5.46*
$\beta_{CK} = \beta_B = \beta_V = \beta_{AT_1} = 0$	10493.3	7989.45	3.99*

As a result of the enforcement cases, 843.31 mergers, or 5.90 mergers per case, were deterred. The precedent cases deterred 1017.81 mergers, or 37.70 mergers per year. Average deterrence is 13.01 mergers per case, and the total amount of deterrence from the entire bundle of merger enforcement is 68.93 mergers per year. Compared to the weighted version of this model, equation 4-6 attributes slightly more deterrence resulting from antitrust policy.

Including the previous six years in the unweighted cumulative index of relative merger enforcement produced

$$M = -6.31 + \quad .74SP + 5.54PR - 68.24AT_5 \qquad (4\text{-}7)$$
$$(-4.74) \quad (.25)^* \quad (1.03)^* \quad (-26.31)^*$$
$$-17.39CK - 19.94V - 7.56B$$
$$(-6.71)^* \quad (-8.89)^* \quad (-10.5)$$

$$\overline{R}^2 = .43 \qquad F = 6.55^* \qquad RSS = 7887.19$$

As in the weighted version, the coefficients of both the relative enforcement index and the *Von's* and Celler-Kefauver dummy variables have a statistically significant effect. Similarly, as shown in table 4-4, both the precedent cases and enforcement cases, as well as the entire bundle of enforcement, have a statistically significant effect on merger activity.

Table 4-4. F-Tests for the Significance of Merger Enforcement from Equation 4-7

Restriction	Restricted Sum of Squared Residuals	Unrestricted Sum of Squared Residuals	F
$\beta_{CK} = \beta_B = \beta_V = 0$	9277.36	7887.19	3.00*
$\beta_{AT_4} = 0$	8948.70	7887.19	6.86*
$\beta_{CK} = \beta_B = \beta_V = \beta_{AT_1} = 0$	10493.30	7887.19	4.21*

The enforcement cases provide 921.24 mergers deterred over the entire period for an average of 6.45 mergers per case. Precedent cases provide deterrence of 762.9 mergers over the entire period, or 28.22 mergers deterred per year. Total deterrence, then, is 62.34 mergers per year; average deterrence is 11.77 mergers per case. The deterrent value from the enforcement cases, both in absolute terms and relative to deterrence from the precedent cases, is larger in the unweighted than in the weighted version of the model.

A comparison of deterrence from the models discussed above with different weights and lags included is shown in table 4-5.

There is some difference in deterrence estimated from the models both in terms of total deterrence and the deterrence allocated between precedent cases and enforcement cases. However, the general conclusion from this comparison is that the estimated coefficients, and hence deterrence, are not overly sensitive to the lags and their weights included in the index of relative merger enforcement. Although the lags and weights included far from exhaust all of the mathematical possibilities, the results in table 4-5 do seem to indicate that using different "reasonable" lags and weights does not greatly alter the estimates of deterrence.

The indexes of merger enforcement used in models 4-4 through 4-7 implicitly assume a constant rate of marginal deterrence—that is, adding additional merger cases to a given level of merger activity yields a constant amount of additional deterrence. This can be seen by differentiating equation 4-7 with respect to AT_5:

$$\frac{d(M)}{d(AT_5)} = \beta_{AT_5}$$

Table 4-5.   Deterrence from Models with Different Weights and Lags
in the Index of Merger Enforcement

Model	Total Deterrence 1950–76	Deterrence Per Year	Average Deterrence Per Case	Deterrence Per Year From Precedent Cases	Deterrence From Enforcement Cases Per Case
weighted 4-lags	1282.79	47.51	8.98	34.53	2.45
weighted 6-lags	1489.06	55.15	10.42	33.59	4.07
unweighted 4-lags	1861.12	68.93	13.01	37.70	5.90
unweighted 6-lags	1683.14	62.38	11.77	28.22	6.45

An incremental change in merger enforcement changes merger activity by a constant amount—β_{AT_5}—regardless of the level of merger enforcement. An alternative structural form—the natural log of the index of merger enforcement—was used to impose diminishing marginal deterrence on the models. Using this form enables an interpretation of the coefficient of the enforcement variable to measure the rate of diminishing marginal deterrence.

Using the index of relative merger enforcement that includes a four-period weighted lag, the model takes the general form

$$M = \alpha + \beta_1 SP + \beta_2 PR + \beta_3 [\ln (MC4/MA4)] + \beta_4 CK + \beta_5 B + \beta_6 V$$

where ln (MC4/MA4) is the natural log of the index of the cumulative relative merger enforcement. Since

$$\ln (MC4/MA4) = \ln MC - \ln MA$$

the model can be rewritten as

$$M = \alpha + \beta_1 SP + \beta_2 PR + \beta_{31} [\ln MC4] - \beta_{32} [\ln MA4] + \beta_4 CK + \beta_5 B + B_6 V$$

This model was estimated as

$$M = -5.02 + .67SP + 5.38PR - 17.69CK - 14.44B \qquad (4\text{-}8)$$
$$ (-4.67) \quad (.25)^* \quad (.99)^* \quad (-6.86)^* \quad (-10.58)$$

$$- 26.22V - 13.49\ln MC4 + 4.73\ln MA4$$
$$(-10.17)^* \quad (-6.92)^* \qquad (5.37)$$

$$\overline{R}^2 = .44 \qquad F = 5.84^* \qquad RSS = 7909.84$$

The coefficient of $\ln MC4$ is interpreted as the effect on mergers of an additional case, given a level of cumulative lagged merger activity. Continual equal increases in merger enforcement will have a diminishing negative effect on merger attempts. Although the Celler-Kefauver and *Von's* dummy variables are both statistically significant, neither the coefficients of B nor $\ln MA4$ are significant. Imposing the relevant restrictions and computing the appropriate F-tests reveals that the relative enforcement variables, $\ln MC4$ and $\ln MA4$, do significantly affect merger activity (see table 4-6). Similarly, an F-test shows that the precedent cases also significantly affect merger activity.

Table 4-6.   F-Tests for the Significance of Merger Enforcement from Equation 4-8

Restriction	Restricted Sum of Squared Residuals	Unrestricted Sum of Squared Residuals	F
$\beta_{CK} = \beta_B = \beta_V = 0$	9735.65	7909.84	3.85*
$\beta_{1nMA4} = \beta_{1nMC4} = 0$	8948.70	7909.84	3.28*
$\beta_{1nMA4} = \beta_{1nMC4} = $ $\beta_{CK} = \beta_B = \beta_V = 0$	10493.30	7909.84	3.27*

As a result of the enforcement cases, 1025.11 mergers were deterred, or 7.17 mergers per case. The precedent cases deterred 937.88 cases or 34.74 mergers per year. Average deterrence is 13.72 mergers per case, or 72.20 mergers per year. The estimated coefficients of the dummy variables are not radically different between the log version of the model estimated in equation 4-8 and the non-log version of the model tested in equation 4-4; therefore deterrence from the precedent cases does not differ greatly between the two models. A slightly greater amount of total deterrence is attributed to antitrust in the log version because of the large effect of enforcement cases on merger activity.

A similar model with the substitution of six, instead of four, weighted lags in the cumulative index of relative merger enforcement was estimated. This produced

$$M = -5.05 + .66SP + 5.42PR - 17.46\,CK - 17.53B \qquad (4\text{-}9)$$
$$\quad\;\; (-4.63) \quad (.24)^* \quad (1.00)^* \quad (-6.90)^* \quad (-10.32)$$

$$-25.3V - 16.53\ln MC6 + 6.08\ln MA6$$
$$(-9.8)^* \quad (-8.26)^* \qquad (6.17)$$

$$\overline{R}^2 = .44 \qquad F = 5.84^* \qquad RSS = 7921.68$$

Unlike its predecessor, equation 4-9 exhibits a statistically significant effect of enforcement cases on merger activity. As shown in table 4-7, both the precedent cases and the relative enforcement variables, as well as the entire bundle of antitrust enforcement, have a statistically significant effect on mergers.

Table 4-7. F-Tests for the Significance of Merger Enforcement from Equation 4-9

Restriction	Restricted Sum of Squared Residuals	Unrestricted Sum of Squared Residuals	F
$\beta_{CK} = \beta_B = \beta_V = 0$	9831.79	7921.68	4.02*
$\beta_{1nMA6} = \beta_{1nMC6} = 0$	8948.70	7921.68	3.24*
$\beta_{1nMA6} = \beta_{1nMC6} =$ $\beta_{CK} = \beta_B = \beta_V = 0$	10493.30	7921.68	3.63*

Deterrence from the enforcement cases is 998.58 mergers, or 6.98 mergers per case. Deterrence from the precedent cases is 968.77 mergers, or 35.88 mergers per year. Total deterrence is 72.86 mergers per year, average deterrence is 13.76 mergers per case.

Marginal Deterrence

The log form used in equation 4-9 enables estimates of marginal deterrence—the amount of deterrence from the last case undertaken (this is discussed in more detail in chapter 3). In equation 4-9 the marginal case in period t affects deterrence in period t+1 in two ways—by increasing the cumulative number of enforcement cases and by decreasing the number of mergers included in the cumulative index of lagged merger activity. That is,

$$M_{t+1} = f(\gamma_{t+1}, P_{t+1}, MC6_t, MA6_t)$$

where γ represents the control variables and P represents the precedent cases.

Since the marginal case in period t affects merger attempts in period $t+1$, the cumulative index of lagged merger activity in period $t+1$ is similarly affected, or $MA6_{t+1} = g(MC6_t)$. In fact, because of the lag structure inherent in MA6, a change in merger enforcement in period t will alter the index of lagged merger activity in the following six periods. Therefore, an incremental change in merger enforcement affects merger activity both directly and indirectly through subsequent changes in the index of cumulative merger activity.

The effect of a small change in merger enforcement on merger attempts can be expressed as

$$\frac{d(M)}{d(MC6)} = \frac{d(\gamma, P, MC6, MA6)}{d(MC6)}$$

Since the function is additive

$$\frac{d(M)}{d(MC6)} = \left(\frac{\partial(\gamma)}{\partial(MC6)} \times \frac{\partial(M)}{\partial(\gamma)} \right) + \left(\frac{\partial(P)}{\partial(MC6)} \times \frac{\partial(M)}{\partial(P)} \right)$$

$$+ \left(\frac{\partial(M)}{\partial(MC6)} \right) + \left(\frac{\partial(MA6)}{\partial(MC6)} \times \frac{\partial(M)}{\partial(MA6)} \right)$$

The control variables and precedent case dummy variables presumably are unaffected by changes in MC:

$$\frac{\partial(\gamma)}{\partial(MC6)} = \frac{\partial(P)}{\partial(MC6)} = 0$$

Given

$$M = \alpha + \beta_\gamma \gamma + \beta_P P + \beta_{\ln MC6} \ln MC6 + \beta_{\ln MA6} \ln MA6$$

then

$$\frac{d(M)}{d(MC6)} = \beta_{lnMC6} \times \frac{1}{MC6} + \beta_{lnMA6} \times \frac{1}{MA6} \times \frac{d(MA6)}{d(MC6)}$$

Marginal deterrence is therefore comprised of two effects—the enforcement effect, $D_E = (\beta_{lnMC6})(1/MC6)$ and the merger index effect, $D_M = \beta_{lnMA6} \times 1/MA6 \times d(MA6)/d(MC6)$. By adding the deterrence from the enforcement effect with the deterrence from the merger index effect, marginal deterrence is approximated

$$D = D_E + D_M$$

Marginal deterrence can be measured from two perspectives—from the perspective of deterrence contributed by the last case undertaken each year, given the historical record of antitrust enforcement, and from the perspective of the deterrence contributed by undertaking additional cases, given a fixed level of hypothetical merger activity. The first perspective enables an estimation of the benefits accruing from any actual case undertaken by the antitrust agencies since the passage of the Celler-Kefauver Act. The second perspective enables identification of the optimal level of merger enforcement—how many cases should be undertaken before the gain from the last case equals the marginal cost of undertaking that case.

The deterrence contributed by the marginal case for each year from 1956 to 1970 is shown in table 4-8 and figure 4-1. Deterrence from the marginal case after 1970 cannot be determined since the marginal deterrence from a case in 1971 includes the effect on the index of merger activity in 1977, for which there is no information. The deterrent value from the marginal case is relatively high in the first two years and then stabilizes around two mergers deterred in subsequent years. This can be interpreted as meaning that if all other historical antitrust enforcement had occurred, except for the marginal case, the additional number of mergers listed in table 4-8 for that year would have occurred. Thus, table 4-8 indicates the value added, in terms of deterrence, from the marginal case undertaken each year. Marginal deterrence with respect to the historical record of antitrust enforcement is not a smooth function. This is because no regular pattern exists either in the annual number of cases brought by the agencies, or the amount of merger activity each year.

Marginal deterrence is a smooth function if two conditions exist: (1) a constant pattern of enforcement, and (2) a constant level of merger activity. At what rate does marginal deterrence diminish as additional

Table 4-8. Marginal Deterrence Over Time

Year	D_E*	D_M**	D***
1956	2.10	1.20	3.30
1957	.90	.56	1.46
1958	1.21	.78	1.99
1959	1.23	.86	2.09
1950	1.35	.97	2.33
1961	.91	.69	1.60
1962	.88	.73	1.61
1963	1.33	1.16	2.49
1964	1.23	1.12	2.35
1965	1.05	.85	1.90
1966	.89	.73	1.62
1967	1.21	1.01	2.22
1968	1.00	.77	1.77
1969	.90	.60	1.50
1970	.82	.55	1.37

* deterrence from enforcement effect

** deterrence from merger index effect

*** marginal deterrence

Figure 4-1.   Marginal Deterrence Over Time

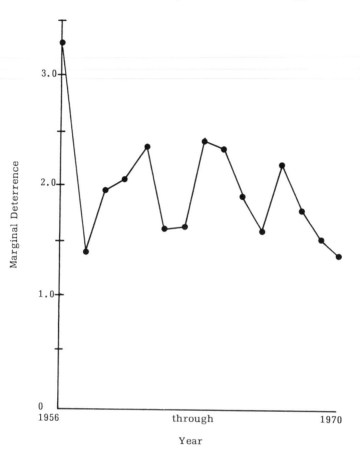

cases are undertaken, given a fixed level of merger activity? This is shown in table 4-9 where the marginal deterrence from additional cases, given a level of six large horizontal mergers occurring annually, or MA6 = 17.64, or lnMA6 = 2.86, is listed. As can be seen in figure 4-2, using the log of the cumulative index of relative merger enforcement does impose diminishing marginal deterrence in equation 4-9; adding cases to a given level of merger activity yields a diminishing amount of additional deterrence. Thus, additional cases increase the total deterrent value from antitrust, but at a decreasing rate. Total deterrence, TD, for different levels of merger enforcement, given MA6 = 17.64, is measured by

$$TD = (\beta_{CK} \times CK) + (\beta_B \times B) + (\beta_V \times V)$$
$$+ (\beta_{lnMC6} \times lnMC6)$$

Table 4-9. Diminishing Marginal Deterrence Given MA6=17.64

MC6	D_E	D_M	D
2	11.46	15.65	27.11
3	6.70	7.87	14.57
4	4.76	5.32	10.07
5	3.69	4.03	7.72
6	3.01	3.24	6.26
7	2.55	2.71	5.26
8	2.21	2.34	4.54
9	1.95	2.05	4.00
10	1.74	1.83	3.57
11	1.58	1.65	3.22
12	1.44	1.50	2.94
13	1.32	1.38	2.70
14	1.23	1.27	2.50
15	1.14	1.18	2.32
16	1.07	1.10	2.17
17	1.00	1.04	2.04
18	.94	.97	1.92

Figure 4-2.   Diminishing Marginal Deterrence Given MA6=17.64

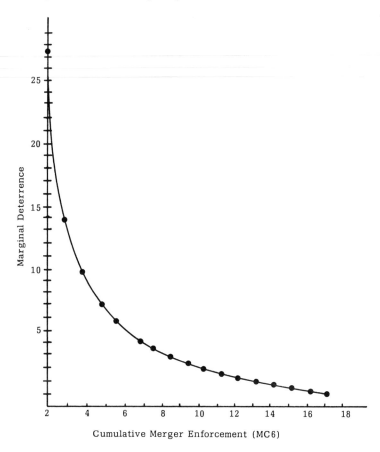

Cumulative Merger Enforcement (MC6)

Selecting increasing levels of merger enforcement yields increasing levels of total deterrence as shown in table 4-10. Figure 4-3 illustrates that total deterrence increases with additional cases, but at a decreasing rate of increase.

Conclusion

The information gained from the models including antitrust variables can be used to make inferences about which of the models not including antitrust variables (4-1 through 4-3) is most reliable. Table 4-11 compares the estimated coefficients of the control variables—SP and PR—for all of the estimated regressions. The control variables are of special interest

Table 4-10. Total Deterrence for Different Levels of Merger
            Enforcement, Given MA6=17.64

MC6	Total Deterrence
2	87.40
3	101.97
4	112.04
5	119.76
6	126.02
7	131.28
8	135.82
9	139.82
10	143.39
11	146.61
12	149.55
13	152.25
14	154.75
15	157.07
16	159.24
17	161.28
18	163.20

Figure 4-3.   Total Deterrence Given MA6=17.64

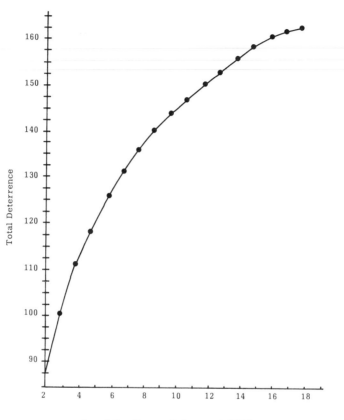

Cumulative Merger Enforcement (MC6)

in the first three regressions because the coefficient of each control variable multipled by the value of the variable during the extrapolated period determines the predicted amount of merger activity in the absence of horizontal merger enforcement, and therefore the deterrent value from antitrust. Presumably, the coefficient of each control variable should be approximately equal between models estimating a pre-merger enforcement period and models including antitrust variables that span the entire period, 1919-76. Because of the presence of effective horizontal merger enforcement, the simple correlation coefficient between merger activity and the control variables is not likely to be the same between ineffective and effective merger enforcement periods. By including antitrust variables in the model, the "net" relationship between the control variables and merger activity should not change between the regimes of ineffective and effective merger enforcement.

The coefficient of PR is larger in the regressions without antitrust variables included. The regression using 1950 as the critical year (4-3), estimated a coefficient for PR considerably larger than its counterpart in the models including antitrust variables (4-4 through 4-9). Similarly, the coefficient of SP in equation 4-3 is radically larger than in any other regression. These inflated values of the coefficients of SP and PR suggest that 1950 is not the critical year representing a change in regimes from ineffective to effective merger enforcement.

Table 4-11. Comparison of Coefficients of the Control Variables for Different Regressions

Regression	SP	PR	Description
4-1	.83	6.64*	1919-1954
4-2	.28	5.58*	1919-1961
4-3	2.66*	7.38*	1919-1949
4-4	.54*	5.10*	weighted, four-lag index
4-5	.66*	5.27*	weighted, six-lag index
4-6	.85*	5.35*	unweighted, four-lag index
4-7	.74	5.54*	unweighted, six-lag index
4-8	.67*	5.38*	weighted, log four-lag index
4-9	.66*	5.42*	weighted, log six-lag index

*Significant for 95% level of confidence

The coefficient of SP in the regression using 1962 as the critical year, equation 4-2, is small relative to all other regressions, and the coefficient of PR is small relative to the other two models not including antitrust variables. Further, SP is not statistically significant in equation 4-2. The weakness of this variable in this regression might be accounted for by the thirteen years after 1949 that include some influence of merger enforcement. Since most of the antitrust variables are excluded from this model, the relationship between SP and merger activity is "washed out" during the period 1950 to 1961.

Using information from regressions 4-4 through 4-9 suggests that 1955 probably best represents the switch from ineffective to effective horizontal merger enforcement. The deterrence measured from equation 4-1, as well as all of the regressions including antitrust variables, is shown in table 4-12. These measures of deterrence will be used in chapter 6 to measure the indirect benefits of merger enforcement.

Table 4-12.   Deterrence from Estimated Models

Regression	Deter- rence Per Year from Precedent Cases	Deterrence from Enforcement Cases Per Case	Average Deter- rence Per Case	Description
4-1	–	–	12.43	1919–1954
4-4	34.53	2.45	8.98	weighted 4-lag index
4-5	33.59	4.07	10.42	weighted 6-lag index
4-6	37.70	5.90	13.01	unweighted 4-lag index
4-7	28.22	6.45	11.77	unweighted 6-lag index
4-8	34.74	7.17	13.72	log weighted 4-lag index
4-9	35.88	6.98	13.76	log weighted 6-lag index

5

The Cost of Horizontal Merger Enforcement

Introduction

Since 1950 the antitrust agencies have issued over 400 complaints challenging over 1,000 acquisitions with combined assets exceeding $20 billion.[1] Table 5-1 shows the extent of merger enforcement, classified according to the primary industry of the acquiring industry, for 1951 through 1977.

Most of the enforcement has been oriented towards preventing horizontal acquisitions. Table 5-2 shows the distribution of large mergers challenged in mining and manufacturing by type of merger, from 1951 to 1977. Large mergers are defined as those involving acquired assets of $10 million or more.

What has been the cost of this antitrust effort? Has it been worth the benefits gained? The magnitude of costs is of grave concern to the antitrust agencies and to Congress. Attorney General Griffin Bell cited high expense, largely due to the court time involved, as a reason for the difficulty involved in enforcing the antitrust laws:

> The weakness in the antitrust system is that it is easy to beat the system. The court processes are so complicated, and so slow, that once a case starts it never seems to end. All you do is just stay in court. You can go on for years in court without anything being done. As long as the court system is not adequate to finish a case within a reasonable time, it is difficult to enforce the antitrust laws.[2]

The purpose of this chapter is to determine the cost of undertaking a horizontal merger case. This will enable a comparison with the benefits accruing from this aspect of Celler-Kefauver enforcement. Measurements of the resources expended by the antitrust agencies will estimate both the average and marginal costs of undertaking a merger case.

Table 5-1. Number of Merger Complaints Issued During 1951-77, By Primary Industry of Acquiring Company

Year of Complaint	Mining and Manu-facturing	Wholesale and Retail	Financial Insti-tutions	Other[1]	Total
1951	0	0	0	0	0
1952	1	0	0	0	1
1953	0	0	0	0	0
1954	2	0	0	0	2
1955	8	0	0	1	9
1956	16	0	0	1	17
1957	7	0	0	1	8
1958	7	0	0	1	8
1959	6	3	1	2	12
1960	20	3	0	1	24
1961	12	1	4	2	19
1962	7	3	2	1	13
1963	8	0	2	1	12
1964	17	1	2	1	21
1965	20	4	2	1	27
1966	15	5	4	2	26
1967	14	0	3	1	18
1968	21	3	10	1	35
1969	19	2	9	1	31
1970	11	1	7	4	23
1971	16	2	11	4	33
1972	15	1	6	3	25
1973	12	2	6	3	23
1974	12	1	2	2	17
1975	7	1	0	1	9
1976	8	3	1	2	14
1977	7	1	1	1	10
Total	289	37	73	38	337

[1]Includes 9 joint ventures.

Source: Willard F. Mueller, "The Celler-Kefauver Act: The First 27 Years," p. 113.

The FTC

One of the difficulties of assigning enforcement costs to a particular antitrust statute is that the agencies initiate complaints and investigate matters covering a wide array of alleged violations. For example, table 5-3 shows the distribution of FTC complaints for different violations over a recent four-year period.

During this period, mergers involved only twenty-one per cent of the FTC complaints. Since all of the antitrust enforcement at the FTC emanates from the Bureau of Competition, a first approximation of resources

Table 5-2. Numbers of Large Acquisitions Challenged in Mining and
Manufacturing By Type of Merger, 1951-77

Type of Merger	1951-1955	1956-1960	1961-1965	1966-1970	1971-1977	Total
Horizontal	5	23	30	34	26	118
Vertical	5	12	9	5	3	34
Conglomerate	5	5	8	13	7	38
Market Extension	3	2	2	3	0	10
Product Extension	2	3	5	8	6	24
Other	0	0	1	2	1	4
Total	15	40	47	52	36	190

Note: Large mergers are defined as those involving
acquired assets of $10,000,000 or more.

Source: Willard F. Mueller, "The Celler-Kefauver Act: The First 27 Years," p. 113.

Table 5-3. FTC Complaints, May 1974-July 1978

Complaint	Cases
Merger	25 (21%)
Horizontal Restrains	18 (15%)
Vertical Restraint	14 (12%)
Monopolization	9 (8%)
Discrimination	25 (21%)
Tying	4 (3%)
Interlock	16 (14%)
Other	6 (5%)
Total	117 (99%)

Source: Office of the Secretary, FTC.

expended on merger activity would be twenty-one per cent of the Bureau's budget. However, this would assume that the total amount of resources spent on each violation is proportional to the number of complaints initiated. Such an assumption is surely erroneous. Monopolization cases involve a great amount of investigation and preparation time as well as court time. Because of the rule of reason criterion used by the courts, these cases are likely to incur large costs per complaint. Price-fixing cases, however, are per se illegal, and probably require considerably less court and investigation time. Therefore, the distribution of FTC complaints by violation does not yield the exact information needed to identify costs per type of case.

Another difficulty in measuring antitrust enforcement expenses is determining what activities should be included. There are many resources used by the agencies besides the time spent in litigation. These costs can be identified by examining the process of case selection at the antitrust agencies.

The Bureau of Competition is responsible for all antitrust matters at the Federal Trade Commission, as previously stated. There are three major stages that matters undergo when being considered by the Bureau. The first is when they are brought to the attention of the FTC. The second is the investigation stage authorized either by the Merger Screening Committee for matters concerning acquisitions and consolidations or by the Evaluation Committee for all other antitrust matters. The third stage involves an official FTC complaint—either a docketed case which is heard before an Administrative Law Judge or a consent order.

In fiscal year 1977 there were 2,157 written matters alleging antitrust violations received by the Bureau of Competition. About sixty per cent of these were from the public or businesspersons and forty per cent were from members of Congress. Further, there are approximately ten complaints by phone per day, adding another 2,600 complaints. Thus, in a given year, the Bureau receives in the neighborhood of 4,800 complaints. The written matters are read by an attorney and the author generally receives a written response. In 1978 one attorney handled a large portion of the written complaints and the ensuing correspondence, as well as most of the phone calls. The matters were reviewed by her, sometimes in consultation with other staff attorneys. She reported that most of the matters involved protection of competitors and were authored by small businesspersons.[3]

Of these matters, a very small percentage get forwarded to the Evaluation and Merger Screening Committees. Cases also reach the Committees from internal sources—attorneys working on related cases, and industry-wide investigations. An Associate Director of the Evaluation

Committee said that the majority of the matters before the Committees have external sources. The Committee, he felt, reacted to complaints from consumers and competitors and rarely approves a proposal based on staff initiation.

Since the 1976 Hart-Scott-Rodino Amendment, all large acquisitions must be reported to the FTC. However, during the period for the data used in this study, no such information mechanism was available at the Commission.

The Evaluation Committee usually meets once a month, and the Merger Screening Committee assembles on a weekly basis. Members of these Committees include staff attorneys and economists from the Bureau of Economics. There is no written criterion for opening an investigation. There exists, however, more or less of a consensus of important factors considered in the decision on whether to investigate a matter. These include apparent illegality, appropriateness of FTC involvement, economic significance, cost to the FTC, impact on the consumer, and the existence of a viable remedy.

If it is deemed appropriate by the Committee, a preliminary investigation is opened to further pursue a matter. After obtaining more information about the alleged violation, the preliminary investigation is closed. If the matter warrants continued analysis, a formal investigation is authorized. If the issue does not seem to merit additional inspection by the Bureau, the matter is dropped.

When sufficient evidence is gathered to instigate a bona fide case, the case is sent to the Commissioners and a formal complaint is issued by the FTC. The matter then takes the form of either a "docketed" or "consent" case. A docketed case is litigated before an Administrative Law Judge. A consent order is a mutually agreeable settlement between the Commission and the defendant.

Table 5-4 shows the number of formal investigations that emerged from those preliminary investigations that were approved and subsequently closed by the Merger Screening Committee, for fiscal years 1975-78. These investigations are categorized by the degree of concentration in the industry of the acquiring firm.

To summarize, a matter must go through the stages of evaluation, shown in figure 5-1, to become an FTC complaint. The cost of bringing a case includes not only‧ the resources expended in the preliminary and formal investigations, as well as litigation costs, but also the cost of searching through much pertinent data to find a feasible case. This would incorporate the time spent on preliminary and formal investigations that were closed and pursued no further.

Table 5-4.   Preliminary and Formal Investigations Approved by the
Merger Screening Committee, July 1975-May 1978

Four-Firm Concentration Ratio	Preliminary Investigations Opened**	Cases from Column 2 Approved for Formal Investigation***
90 - 100	0 (0%)	0 (0%)
80 - 89	1 (1%)	1 (4%)
65 - 79	6 (8%)	4 (15%)
50 - 64	25 (32%)	7 (28%)
35 - 49	24 (31%)	6 (24%)
20 - 34	10 (13%)	1 (4%)
0 - 19	12 (15%)	6 (24%)
Total	78 (100%)	25 (100%)

**Excludes preliminary investigations still open.
***All remaining preliminaries were closed.

Source: Office of the Secretary, FTC.

The number of hours expended by the FTC staff on all of the stages of a case for every matter investigated by the FTC from July 1974 to May 1978 was obtained from the Office of the Secretary at the FTC, in "The Allocation of Antitrust Resources," an unpublished working paper written by this author at the General Accounting Office in 1978. In facilitating the G.A.O. study, the Inquiry and Search branch of the Information Division at the FTC made available the time allocation of antitrust resources.

Time at the Bureau of Competition is accounted for in terms of inception-to-date (ITD) hours. This includes not only attorney time, but also the number of hours expended by members of Economic Evidence, general staff, and Administrative Law Judges. Even though the sample period begins in 1974, the ITD hours for any matter still open at that time, but initiated in an earlier year, include the time spent commencing with the inception of the preliminary investigation. Thus, ITD hours cover almost the entire history of the matter.

The time devoted to a merger case can be obtained from the ITD hours allocated to docketed and consent cases that were closed during the sample period. All of these cases are listed in table 5-5, along with the docket or consent number, alleged violation, and the ITD hours.

Figure 5-1.   The Stages of Case Selection, FTC

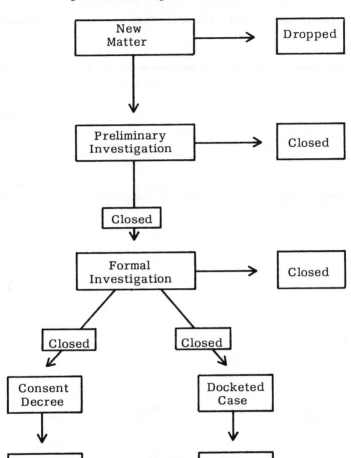

The number of FTC staff hours expended varies considerably between cases. The *American Bakeries* case consumed only 100 ITD hours; over 400 times that amount of resources was devoted to *Beatrice Foods,* which lists an ITD of 41,054 hours. The mean ITD for the entire sample is 10,110.3 hours, with a standard deviation of 12,048.9 hours.

Horizontal merger cases were not separated from the rest of the sample for several reasons. First, only one complaint, *Cargill Inc.,* does not explicitly involve two competitors merging. The violation category "mergers" is a broad catchall classification, including all possible types of acquisitions and consolidations. Second, much of the investigation and litigation time in a merger case revolves around defining the market. Often a case may not emerge as a distinct type until after considerable investigation. Thus, cases may be included in the "mergers" classification if the type of merger is not readily apparent at the time the preliminary investigation is authorized. Clearly it would be inappropriate to treat the cost of undertaking a pure conglomerate case as being similar to the cost of a horizontal merger case. However, this issue does not arise here because of the absence of any pure conglomerate cases in the sample.

Table 5-5.   Docket and Consent Merger Cases Closed by the FTC, July 1974-May 1978

Defendant	Case Number	Violation	ITD Hours
ABC Consolidated Corporation	D7652	Horizontal Mergers	19413
Allied Stores Corporation	C1001	Mergers	1961
American Bakeries Company	C1111	Mergers	100
Beatrice Foods	D6653	Mergers	41054
Bic Pen Corporation	D9095	Horizontal Mergers	484
Cambell Taggart	D7938	Horizontal Mergers	20527
Budd Company	D8848	Horizontal Mergers	7472
Cargill Inc.	D9005	Vertical and Product Extension Mergers	803
Cole National Corporation	D8701	Mergers	2564
Dean Foods	D8674	Mergers	9251
E. J. Korvette	C1106	Horizontal Mergers	4730
Food Town Stores, Inc.	D9087	Horizontal and Market Extension Mergers	1402
Foremost Dairies, Inc.	D6495	Horizontal Mergers	16210
Fruehauf Trailer Company	D6608	Horizontal Mergers	23414
Lone Star Cement	C1159	Horizontal Mergers	1518
May Department Stores	C1105	Mergers	2600
National Tea Company	D7453	Horizontal Mergers	25561

(Continued)

Table 5-5

(continued)

Defendant	Case Number	Violation	ITD Hours
Proctor and Gamble	C1169	Mergers	4751
Rexall Drug and Chemical	C1252	Mergers	2657
Standard Oil of Ohio	D8910	Mergers	15092
Union-Bag Camp Paper	D7946	Horizontal Mergers	34838

Source: Office of the Secretary, FTC.

In addition to the hours expended directly on each complaint, a great deal of time was invested to find these cases. How much time is spent searching for the average case? The ideal procedure for answering this question would be to examine all of the preliminary investigations authorized in a given period of time. The number of matters that ultimately got approved to the litigation or consent stage would constitute the output from that period. The number of hours spent on investigations that were subsequently dropped with no further action by the Commission would be considered as the cost of searching for cases. All of the hours spent on new matters examined by the FTC during the sample period would be accounted for as belonging either to the output—a docketed case or a consent decree—or to the cost of searching.

Unfortunately, this ideal procedure is not feasible given the sample period. Many of the cases that were opened as preliminary investigations in 1974 to 1977 were still open as formal investigations at the close of the period. It could not be ascertained if the hours expended on these matters would be towards an official complaint or search cost. Further, it will be years before all of the docketed and consent cases are finished. Thus, there is no way of determining the total number of hours spent on them.

It is possible to obtain an estimate of average search cost per case, and therefore the entire enforcement cost, for the cases listed in table 5-5 by making several assumptions about the flow of agency activity over the case-selection cycle. The case-selection cycle can be divided into three components—preliminary investigation, formal investigation, and FTC complaint status—as shown in figure 5-2.

If (1) the FTC spends the same number of hours on preliminary investigations in any comparable sample period; (2) the same proportion, in terms of ITD hours, or prelims are approved for formal investigation in each period; and (3) the same number of complaints are issued by the FTC each period; then the cost of searching for docketed cases and consent decrees is equal for every period. That is, the same number of ITD hours will be devoted to preliminary and formal investigations closed without further consideration by the Commission in every sample period. This is shown in figure 5-2. To determine the search cost of bringing the twenty-one FTC complaints listed in table 5-5, ITD hours on closed and unpursued preliminary and formal investigations during the 1974-78 sample period should be computed.

Figure 5-2.   Model of the Case Selection Cycle with Constant
Investigations and Search Costs

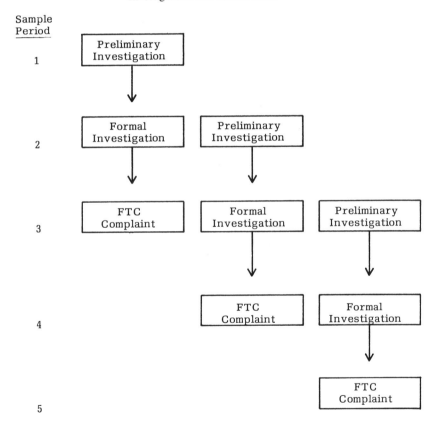

The amount of time devoted to preliminary investigations, P, includes hours spent on matters subsequently given formal investigation status, P_s, and matters abandoned, P_u. Similarly, the amount of time spent on formal investigations, F, is comprised of hours spent on matters ultimately becoming FTC complaints, F_s, and matters dropped, F_u. Therefore, only some of the hours in P_s can be classified as actually spent directly on a case reaching the complaint stage—P_{ss}; the others, P_{su}, become search cost when formal investigations are discarded. So,

$$P_s = P_{ss} + P_{su}$$

In any given sample period, the total hours spent, H, on bringing N complaints is given by

$$H = P + F + C$$

where

$$P = P_s + P_u$$
$$F = F_s + F_u$$

and C is the hours spent on docket and consent cases. The total number of hours expended per case, MC, is

$$MC = H/N$$

The direct cost per case—the ITD hours associated with only that complaint—is given by DC:

$$DC = \frac{(P_{ss} + F_s + C)}{N}$$

The cost of searching for the N complaints is $P_u + P_{su} + F_u$. The search cost per case, SC, is

$$SC = \frac{(P_u + P_{su} + F_u)}{N}$$

The direct cost plus search cost equals the total cost per case

$$MC = DC + SC$$

or

$$MC = \frac{(P_{ss} + F_s + C)}{N} + \frac{(P_u + P_{su} + F_u)}{N}$$

The direct cost per case, DC, has already been determined as 10,110.3 FTC staff hours. During 1974 to 1978, 105 separate matters were considered and dropped by the Commission without further attention. Only twenty-three of these matters accumulated ITD time exceeding 100 hours. The ITD time for these 105 matters was 92,450 hours. That is,

$$92,450 = P_u + P_{su} + F_u$$

An average of 880.47 hours was devoted to each matter.

Search cost per case, SC, is 4,402.4 hours. Total hours—direct plus search—is 14,512.70 per case. Since these hours include only time spent directly pertaining to the case, and do not incorporate administrative overhead, such as the operations of the Evaluation and Merger Screening Committees, this measure approximates marginal cost.

So far the discussion has referred to costs in terms of ITD hours. This measure can be converted into a dollar value. As described earlier, ITD hours include the time expended by attorneys, economists, staff, and Adminstrative Law Judges on antitrust enforcement. Ideally, the average hourly wage of each group could be weighted by their hours spent on antitrust matters to determine a composite dollar value for a unit of ITD.

The only information available from the FTC is that, on average, an attorney earned approximately $35,000, or $17.50 per hour in 1979. Assigning this figure to each unit of ITD time may not be too inaccurate. Certainly much of the staff's income is less than the average attorney's salary; however, the income of an Administrative Law Judge is presumably higher than the average attorney's salary. Perhaps these two factors are somewhat offsetting.

In 1979 dollars, the total hours expended per case multiplied by the average hourly wage rate paid to attorneys, yields the cost per case— $253,972. There are also costs to the Government beyond what is included in this figure. For example, overhead and administrative costs, such as those incurred by the Evaluation and Merger Screening Committees, as well as Congressional time spent debating the antitrust laws, and appeals to the Federal Courts, might all be considered to impose additional demands on public resources.

It is possible to allocate some of the administrative costs of operating the section of the FTC responsible for antitrust enforcement—the Bureau of Competition—to merger enforcement. In the fiscal year 1980, the budget for the Bureau was $15,427,000. The Bureau estimates that 16.5 per cent of ITD hours are spent on merger activity. If administrative costs are assumed to be proportional to the amount of enforcement for each type of violation, then $2,545,455 will be allocated to enforcing the Celler-Kefauver Amendment. Since twenty-one merger complaints were completed during the four-year sample period, the number of expected merger cases occurring annually is approximately 5.25. To bring a merger complaint costs the Bureau of Competition $484,849. This figure approximately measures the average cost of a case since it includes at least the largest fixed costs. The figure of $253,972 more closely approximates the marginal cost of a merger case.

The Relationship Between Acquiring Firm Size and Enforcement Costs

In the previous section, measures of marginal and average costs per case were derived. These costs will be compared to the marginal and average benefits accruing from merger enforcement. Inspection of table 5-5 shows a large variance in the ITD hours expended on each complaint. Therefore, several hypotheses are tested concerning the relationship between the amount of time spent on a case, and characteristics of the acquiring firm. If a statistically significant relationship could be found between the cost of a case and specific firm attributes, a much more accurate assignment of costs could be made for cases not included in the sample period. Also, knowledge of such a relationship would be extremely useful in implementing antitrust policy.

The twenty-one cases listed in table 5-5 do not constitute a very large sample from which to make statistical inferences using regression analysis. This deficiency was remedied. Also included in the data are consent and docketed cases that were still open as of May 1978. However, many of these cases were closed shortly after this time. Also, some of the complaints had already undergone the most time-consuming aspects of their tenure—investigation and litigation. These cases require only minimal attention from the Commission, since they are in a compliance state. Therefore, twelve of the consent and docketed cases still open were added to the original sample in table 5-5. The selection criterion for these complaints was a minimum of 1,200 accumulated ITD hours.

Since none of these cases were completed, it was expected that the mean ITD hours of the open cases would be substantially less than the average for the closed cases. In fact, for the open cases, the mean ITD is 9988.3—only 121.97 hours per case less than the average for closed cases. Hence, the understatement of costs for the sample of open cases seems to be minimal. The cases included in the sample that were still open as of May 1978 are listed in table 5.6.

Table 5-6.   Docket and Consent Merger Cases Still Open at the FTC, May 1978

Defendant	Case Number	Violation	ITD Hours
Borg-Warner Corporation	C2716	Horizontal Mergers	1640
Damon Corporation	C2916	Horizontal Mergers	14842
Atlantic Richfield	D9089	Horizontal, Vertical and Product Extension Mergers	19640
Federal-Mogul Corporation	D9046	Vertical Mergers	14312
Harnischfeger	D9107	Horizontal Mergers	1112
Kaiser Aluminum Chemical	D9080	Horizontal Mergers	11777
Kennecott Copper	D8765	Mergers	3348
Lancaster Colony Corporation	D9101	Horizontal Mergers	2833
Pillsbury Company	D9091	Horizontal and Market Extension Mergers	10337
Reichold Chemicals	D9076	Horizontal Mergers	6928
Standard Oil of Indiana	C2770	Horizontal and Vertical Mergers	2645
Tenneco	D9097	Product Extension and Horizontal Mergers	6293

Source: Office of the Secretary, FTC.

The mean ITD time for the combined samples of open and closed complaints is 10,066.0 hours, with a standard deviation of 10,701 hours. It was hypothesized that the number of hours compiled in a case is related to the size of the acquiring firm. This follows from the premise that larger firms have a greater amount of resources available to engage in a legal contest. Thus, in order to achieve equal representation, the enforcement agency must spend more money in its prosecution. A similar relationship was assumed in the paper by Long, Schramm, and Tollison[4] discussed in chapter 2. According to Long, et al., "One way to estimate the costs to the Antitrust Division indirectly is to estimate the industry resources available to fight or prolong antitrust action against the industry."[5]

Two measures of firm size were used—assets and sales. Data on the assets of the acquiring firms were obtained from *Moody's* and *The Merger Case Digest.*[6] The sales data were obtained from *The Merger Case Digest* and the EIS. Information about size was available only for twenty-seven of the thirty-three firms in the sample.

The hypothesized linear relationship was estimated as

$$ITD = 9156.99 + .029A \qquad (5\text{-}1)$$
$$(2217.93)^* \quad (.223)$$

$$R^2 = .001 \qquad F = .025 \qquad RSS = 232078 \times 10^4$$

where ITD is the total hours spent on the complaint, and A is the assets of the acquiring firm for one year preceding the aquisition. Clearly, there is no relationship at all between the assets of an acquiring firm and the resources spent by the FTC in that case.

The natural log of the acquiring firm's assets was used as an explanatory variable to test if the size of the firm exhibited a diminishing influence on the amount of resources allocated by the FTC to that case. This produced

$$ITD = 7765.29 + 205.364LA \qquad (5\text{-}2)$$
$$(9514.74) \quad (1235.76)$$

$$R^2 = .001 \qquad F = .025 \qquad RSS = 23198 \times 10^5$$

where LA is the natural log of assets of the acquiring firm in the merger case. As in its predecessor, equation 5-2 shows there is no statistically significant relationship between ITD and firm size as measured by assets.

Using sales to measure firm size did not alter the results from the previous equations. The linear relationship was estimated as

$$ITD = 10123.10 - .0536S \qquad (5\text{-}3)$$
$$(2192.74)^* \quad (-.111)$$

$$R^2 = .009 \qquad F = .227 \qquad RSS = 234628 \times 10^4$$

where S is the amount of total sales of the acquiring firm. Once again, the variation in the variable measuring size explains virtually none of the variation in ITD.

From equations 5-1 through 5-3, it can be concluded that the size of the acquiring firm, as measured either by assets or sales, has no influence on the amount of resources spent by the FTC on a merger case. Thus, the hypothesized relationship between agency enforcement costs and resources available to the acquiring firm is not accepted.

This conclusion is not particularly surprising. A merger between two firms competing in the same product and geographic markets is virtually illegal per se, especially if one of the firms is a leading or dominant firm in the industry. If both the defendant and the Government agree on the definitions of the relevant product and geographic markets, there will be little to contest in court, regardless of the amount of resources available to the defense.

For example, in the *Allied Stores* complaint (C1001), Allied, the second-largest conventional department store chain in the United States, and second-largest in San Antonio, Texas, purchased the fourth-ranking department store in San Antonio—Wolff and Marx. A preliminary investigation was authorized to study the acquisition in October 1965. A complaint was subsequently issued by the Commission on October 8, 1965. That same day a consent order was filed, requiring Allied to divest the retail store, situated in a shopping center in San Antonio, which was acquired from Wolff and Marx.

It appears that in the *Allied Stores* case, the relevant markets alleged by the Commission—department stores in San Antonio—were sufficiently clear that the defendant chose not to contest the matter in litigation. Thus, only 1,961 hours were devoted to the case by the time it was closed in 1975.

In some horizontal merger cases, however, such as *United States v. Bethlehem Steel Corp.*[7] and *United States v. Philadelphia National Bank,*[8] defining the market is very controversial. In these cases a considerable amount of time in court is devoted to hearing arguments and testimony from expert witnesses concerning the degree of competition between the merging firms.

The Commission's complaint against *Fruehauf Trailer Co.* (D6608) involved a contested product market definition. Fruehauf, which acquired several firms producing various types of trailers, averred that the relevant market included not only the sale of truck trailers but also trucks and other transportation equipment. The Government disputed this definition and argued that van trailers, dump trailers, platform trailers, and tank trailers each constituted a separate line of commerce and aluminum van trailers a sub-line of commerce where competition may be substantially lessened.

The Commission held that the acquisitions of two of the firms, Strick and Hobbs, were unlawful. In 1966, ten years after the complaint was issued, a divestiture order was filed. When the case was finally closed in 1976, 23,414 hours had been spent investigating and litigating the matter.

Both the *Fruehauf Trailer Co.* and *Allied Stores* complaints involved large defendants and horizontal merger violations. Yet the Commission incurred very different costs for each case. It is the cases with more uncertainty with respect to product and geographic market definitions that are likely to cause greater enforcement expenses for the antitrust agencies. Since there is no reason to expect the size of the acquiring firm to be related to the amount of controversy over the relevant line of commerce, the results from equations 5-1 through 5-3 are not surprising.

It would be interesting to estimate the relationship between agency enforcement costs and firm characteristics for alleged violations subject to more of a rule of reason by the courts. For example, in a monopolization case, intent to monopolize usually must be inferred by the court to rule against the defendant. Hence, both parties invest a great amount of resources trying to show the existence or lack of such a motive. A relationship between firm size and the agency's cost is more likely to be found for such types of antitrust violations.

From the results of the preceding regressions, there seems to be no a priori basis for assigning costs to cases outside of the sample according to firm attributes. This validates using the average measures of cost on a per case basis that were derived in the previous section.

The Antitrust Division

The measures of cost discussed heretofore are based solely on data from the FTC. The Antitrust Division at the Department of Justice also pursues violations of the amended section 7 of the Clayton Act. Enough information is available to compute the average cost of undertaking a merger case by the Antitrust Division.

The Antitrust Division has grown since its incipience in 1933 from a budget of $142,000 to $31 million in 1978. There were sixteen attorneys at the Division in 1933; by 1978 there were 413 attorneys. In 1978 there were 858 people employed by the Division—413 attorneys, forty-two economists, fifty-nine para-legals, and 344 secretaries and other personnel. Approximately seventy-one per cent of the Division's employees are located in Washington, D.C. The remainder are in the field throughout the nation.[9]

About ten per cent of the Division's resources spent on professionals are allocated to economists. The explanation is:

> The principles underlying the antitrust laws are related directly to issues of economic market structure, conduct and performance. Thus, careful economic analysis is essential to an effective enforcement program. The Economic Policy Office is staffed with professional economists whose skills are used from the preliminary investigation stage through to actual litigation and final judgment enforcement. They provide an early evaluation of the economic significance of business activities proposed for investigation; assist the legal staff by defining relevant markets and analyzing the economic effect of market structure, conduct and performance; and participate in planning and implementing Division intervention in regulatory activities and in designing regulatory reform proposals.[10]

The Office of Operations is responsible for the process of case selection at the Antitrust Division. This office is charged with the responsibility for "ensuring consistency with Division enforcement policy, maintaining quality control over the Division's work product at certain important stages, and avoiding duplication of effort among sections and between the Division and the FTC, and reviews proposed civil and criminal cases recommended by the sections and field offices."[11]

Like the Evaluation and Merger Screening Committees at the Bureau of Competition, the Office of Operations reviews all matters proposed for investigation. There are relatively few denials, usually for reasons such as a small amount of commerce involved, duplication of effort, absence of a viable legal theory, or no apparent violation. If the matter is deemed worthy of further consideration, the Office of Operations assigns a preliminary investigation.

A matter can also be given Civil Investigative Demand (CID) status. This process is similar to subpoena power, but involves a potentially greater amount of resources committed by the Division and therefore requires the endorsement of the Assistant Attorney General: "CID's are reviewed to ensure that they adequately describe the nature of the conduct constituting the alleged violation, are soundly based in legal theory, seek relevant information, and are not so broad as to entail unnecessary burden or expense for the respondent."[12]

Over a recent one-month period, the allocation of Division time for its major activities was:[13]

Civil Litigation	19.0%
Criminal Litigation	6.5
Grand Jury Investigations	20.0
Civil Investigations	5.5
Merger Investigations	7.0
Regulatory Agency Proceedings	6.5
Other Matters	14.0

Resources expended by the Division on merger enforcement include merger investigations along with that portion of civil litigation and civil investigation involved in merger cases. A portion of regulatory agency proceedings and other matters might also be charged to merger enforcement. The classification "other matters" refers to items such as ". . .

Table 5-7. The Allocation of Antitrust Division Resources, October 1975-February 1977

PERSON MONTHS

	Oct. '75 Feb. '77	Oct. '75 Sept. '76	Since Oct. '76 (Thru Feb. '77)
SHERMAN, SECTION 1	3,187 (65.5%)	2,178 (63.2%)	1,009 (71.1%)
(Price Fixing, Horizontal Sellers)	1,745 (36 %)	1,176 (34.1%)	569 (40.2%)
SHERMAN, SECTION 2	600 (12.4%)	425 (12.4%)	174 (12.3%)
SHERMAN, SECTION 3	8	6	2
CLAYTON, SECTION 3	81	61	19
CLAYTON, SECTION 4	106	80	25
CLAYTON, SECTION 7	696 (14.3%)	541 (13 %)	154 (11 %)
CLAYTON, SECTION 8	16	14	2
ROBINSON-PATMAN, SECTION 2	1	.850	.500
OTHER VIOLATIONS OF THE ANTITRUST LAW	165 (3.4%)	136 (4 %)	28 (.02%)

Source: Antitrust Division Violation/Product Summary Report For Matters Reported in the October 1975 to February 1977 Monthly Reports.

time spent by attorneys and economists in training programs and reading to keep abreast of recent court decisions, and industrial and economic developments, participation in intradepartmental or interagency task forces that do not relate to any of our other specific categories of activity, and maintaining liaison with the State Department and various other organizations on international trade matters."[14]

Like the Bureau of Competition, the Antitrust Division maintains records on the amount of time spent on different violations. Table 5-7 shows the allocation of person-months for different categories of antitrust violations during a sixteen-month period (October 1975 to February 1977)[15]; Clayton Act, Section 7 cases, which deal exclusively with mergers, used fourteen per cent of the agency's resources. Based on the 1978 budget, this is an expenditure of $4,340,000 on merger enforcement.

How many cases were brought by the Division as a result of this antitrust activity? Table 5-8 lists recent Department of Justice merger enforcement activity,[16] and table 5-9 lists the cases actually filed between January 1, 1977 and June 30, 1978.[17]

Table 5-8.   Antitrust Division Merger Enforcement Activity, January 1977-June 1978

Filing Date	Mergers Examined By Antitrust Division	Authorized Preliminary Investigations	Cleared to FTC for Investigation	Cases Filed
1/ 1/77-6/30/77	520	41	27	2
7/ 1/77-12/31/77	597	36	25	3
1/ 1/78-6/30/78	621	43	34	3

Source: U.S. Department of Justice.

In this one-year period six cases were brought by the Antitrust Division. The amount of the Division's budget devoted to merger enforcement—$4,340,000—divided by the number of cases brought—six—yields an average cost of $723,333 per case in 1978 dollars.

The average cost calculated for an Antitrust Division case is somewhat higher than the average cost derived for the FTC. This disparity might be accounted for by a differential in the administrative costs at the agencies. The Antitrust Division had a budget more than twice the size of the Bureau of Competition's budget in 1978. Perhaps this indicates that administrative costs at the Division exceed those of the Commission. If so, the average cost per merger case would include a greater amount of fixed costs at the Justice Department than at the FTC. Also, additional overhead at the FTC may occur outside the Bureau of Competition. To the degree this exists, the average cost measure for the FTC derived in this chapter is understated.

Table 5-9. Cases Filed by the Antitrust Division January 1977-June
1978

Filing Date	Case	Disposition as of 6/30/78
5/26/77	U.S. v. Second National Bank and Trust Company of Lexington	Merger Abandoned
6/28/77	U.S. v. Culbro Corp.	Consent
7/ 5/77	U.S. v. United Technologies Corp.	Litigation lost but acquisition fell through
8/15/77	U.S. v. Revco D.S. Inc.	Merger abandoned
12/ 9/77	U.S. v. Alcan Aluminum Limited	Merger abandoned
4/13/78	U.S. v. Consolidated Food Corporation	Appeal being considered
5/10/78	U.S. v. Combustion Engineering	Merger abandoned
6/1/78	U.S. v. Columbia Broadcasting System, Inc.	In litigation

Source: U.S. Department of Justice.

Not all of the cases brought by the Department of Justice and FTC achieve successful decisions, from the perspective of the Government. From his interviews with administrators responsible for the enforcement activities at the Antitrust Division Leonard Weiss,[18] in his paper discussed in chapter 2, attributed a ninety-five per cent probability of success to horizontal merger cases.

Table 5-10 indicates the outcome of all of the merger cases, excluding banks, brought by the antitrust agencies from 1951 to 1977.[19] Unfortunately, these data were not further classified by merger type. Of the 336 completed cases, forty-four were dismissed by the court. This implies a probability of success of eighty-seven per cent for all types of merger cases. An additional twenty-five cases did not attain even partial divestiture. Thus, the probability of obtaining at least some relief is eighty per cent.

As reported in chapter 4, the number of successful horizontal merger

Table 5-10.   Merger Cases (Excluding Banks) Brought by the Department of Justice and Federal Trade Commission, Classified By Status and Extent of Relief, 1951-77

Status or relief	Number of complaints (1)	Percent of complaints (2)	Percent of completed cases (3)	Value of challenged assets (millions) (4)	Percent of challenged assets (5)	Percent of challenged assets in completed cases (6)	Average total assets challenged in complaint (millions) (7)
Case dismissed	44	12	13	$2,331	9	10	$53
Complete divestiture	175	48	53	9,989	38	44	57
Partial divestiture	92	25	27	7,980	30	35	87
No divestiture	25	7	7	2,347	9	10	95
total completed cases	326	92	100	22,648	85	100	67
Pending	28	8 --------		3,959	15 ------------		141
Total	364	100 ---------		26,607	100 ------------		73

Source: Willard F. Mueller, "The Celler-Kefauver Act: The First 27 Years," p. 119.

cases in manufacturing from 1950 to 1974 is 143. Over that same period there were thirteen Antitrust Division and seven FTC cases that were not successful involving horizontal acquisitions in manufacturing industries. Thus, of the horizontal merger cases in manufacturing, twelve per cent were unsuccessful. The probability of success for a horizontal merger case in manufacturing is eighty-eight per cent.

Adjusting the derived cost of the agencies for a horizontal merger case to include the expense of an unsuccessful outcome yields the cost of undertaking a successful case. This is shown in table 5-11.

Table 5-11.   The Cost of Undertaking a Successful Horizontal Merger Case

Measure	Per Case	Per Successful Case
FTC Marginal Cost	$255,000	$290,000
FTC Average Cost	485,000	551,000
Antitrust Division Average Cost	723,000	822,000

Table 5-12.   The Cost of a Horizontal Merger Case, 1954-74

Year	Average Cost	Marginal Cost
1954	$1,488,000	$ 628,000
1955	1,520,000	641,000
1956	1,568,000	662,000
1957	1,621,000	684,000
1958	1,647,000	695,000
1959	1,683,000	710,000
1960	1,712,000	722,000
1961	1,727,000	729,000
1962	1,758,000	742,000
1963	1,783,000	752,000
1964	1,812,000	765,000
1965	1,852,000	782,000
1966	1,913,000	807,000
1967	1,969,000	831,000
1968	2,058,000	868,000
1969	2,161,000	912,000
1970	2,277,000	961,000
1971	2,393,000	1,010,000
1972	2,492,000	1,052,000
1973	2,640,000	1,114,000
1974	2,892,000	1,220,000

**In constant dollars, based on GNP deflator 1972=100

Not all of the economic costs in a merger case are incurred by the Government. It is generally accepted that private costs in a typical case probably exceed those of the antitrust agency.[20] Unfortunately, there is no detailed information available revealing the extent of private expenses in antitrust suits. In his study described in chapter 2, Weiss estimated the ratio of private to public antitrust attorneys to be 5:1. His measure was based on the proportion of government lawyers relative to the number of private attorneys belonging to the Section of Antitrust of the American Bar Association. Although only seventy per cent of the attorneys who have been admitted to the bar are ABA members, not all of the attorneys specializing in antitrust work full time in that area. Weiss suggests that these two biases are approximately offsetting.

Since no additional information is available to improve upon Weiss's estimate, a similar assumption is used in this paper to approximate private costs. Table 5-12 shows the estimates of average and marginal costs, in real dollars, expended on horizontal merger enforcement that will be used throughout the remainder of this study. The average cost is based on the mean of the cost estimates at the Antitrust Division and FTC.

6

The Benefits from Horizontal Merger Enforcement

Introduction

The previous two chapters have estimated the deterrent effect, in terms of numbers of large horizontal mergers, and measured the costs, based on the amount of resources expended by the antitrust agencies, from horizontal merger enforcement. In this chapter the benefits from deterrence, along with the direct gain from each case, will be estimated. These benefits will then be compared with the costs, enabling an evaluation of the economic efficiency of horizontal merger enforcement.

As discussed previously, the major economic benefits from antitrust cases, which were inferred from apparent Congressional intent, are the prevention and elimination of monopoly power causing (1) a redistribution of wealth from consumers to firms, and (2) a loss in allocative efficiency. Using the methodology described in chapter 3, the redistribution and allocative efficiency benefits from enforcement of the Celler-Kefauver Act will be determined under various assumptions about the deterrent effect. Therefore, lower and upper limits of the magnitude of the benefits are derived to compare the gains with the costs, enabling an evaluation of horizontal merger enforcement.

The Redistribution of Wealth

In chapter 3, the net direct benefits from the redistribution of wealth, B_{qd}, from firms to consumers as a result of antitrust policy was derived as

$$B_{qd} = \sum_{n=0}^{N} \left(\frac{(1 - tr)}{(1 + d)^n} \cdot b \cdot VS_a \cdot V_n \right) \tag{6-1}$$

where tr is the corporate tax rate, VS_a is the value of shipments of the acquired firm in the relevant market, N is the duration of effect, and d is the discount rate. From the study by Preston and Collins,[1] b is estimated as 0.144. This indicates the percentage increase in the price-cost margin resulting from a one percent increase in the four-firm concentration ratio due to the merger.

V_n takes on the value of zero in every period prior to divestiture of the consolidated firm, and a value of one in all subsequent periods. That is, given n^* as an index for the year when relief is obtained, if $n^*>n$, $V_n = 0$; if $n^* \leq n$, $V_n = 1$. This reflects the absence of a direct gain without an effective remedy. As Kenneth Elzinga[2] observed in his paper reviewed in chapter 2, when a case is initiated and when effective relief is obtained are not always simultaneous occasions.

Data for the value of shipments of the acquired firm in the relevant market was gathered from a variety of sources—the *Merger Case Digest*,[3] *The Celler-Kefauver Act: The First 27 Years*,[4] and the *Statistical Report: Value of Shipments Data by Product Class for the 1,000 Largest Manufacturing Companies of 1950*.[5] In most cases it was possible to distinguish the value of shipments which the acquired and acquiring firm had in common from the total value of shipments of the acquired firm. The *Merger Case Digest* was especially useful in identifying the share of an acquired firm's sales that were in the same market as the acquiring firm. For example, in a case brought by the Justice Department, *American Radiator and Standard Sanitary Corp.* (C14469), the total sales of the acquired company, Mullins, in the year prior to the acquisition is listed as $59,000,000. But the value of shipments of products that Mullins had in common with American-Standard is also given: "Prior to the merger, American-Standard and Mullins were competitors to the extent that in 1955, the value of shipments by American-Standard of products similar to those shipped by Mullins was $38,294,574, and the value of shipments by Mullins of products similar to those shipped by American-Standard was $49,558,114."[6]

Such exact delineation of overlapping markets of the merged companies was not always available. However, it was usually possible to procure at least an approximation of the value of shipments of the acquired firm in markets which were common to the consolidated firms.

Not all of the cases examined in this chapter obtained effective relief. Clearly it is undesirable to attribute a direct benefit to cases that ultimately allowed the merger to stand, even though the Government won the case. In his paper previously mentioned, Elzinga[7] provided a classification of cases prior to 1960 that enables some identification of those merger cases where adequate relief was not achieved. Those cases which were listed by Elzinga in the category of "unsuccessful relief," based on the independence and viability of the rechartered firm, were assigned zero direct benefits.

Elzinga also classified the cases according to the length of time from the date of the acquisition to the date that divestiture was accomplished. However, this study does not utilize this dimension of effective relief, since the benefits measured by equation 6-1 are discounted.

Unfortunately, no reference analogous to Elzinga's study classifying the effectiveness of relief exists for the years following 1960. In some cases, however, based on information from the *Merger Case Digest* and *The Celler-Kefauver Act: The First 27 Years*, it was obvious that effective relief had not been achieved. For example, in an FTC complaint initiated against *Litton Industries, Inc.* (D-8878), on April 10, 1969, Litton was found to be in violation of the Clayton Act, Section 7. An FTC opinion and order to divest was issued on March 13, 1973. The order requested divestiture of the acquired firm, and a permanent moratorium on all acquisitions of firms manufacturing or selling typewriters, typewriter parts, or accessories. However, this order was modified on March 4, 1975, and Litton was allowed to retain the acquired company.[8] Thus, no direct benefit was assigned to the Litton Industries, Inc. case, or to similar cases that appear to fail in obtaining relief.

The number of years between the filing date of a case and accomplishment of divestiture, n^*, was also identified from the *Merger Case Digest* and *The Celler-Kefauver Act: The First 27 Years*. For example, in an FTC complaint filed on April 30, 1968, against *Stanley Works* (D-8760), it is reported that, "Order extending time to Jan. 27, 1970, to respondents for filing appeal from hearing examiner's initial decision to cease and desist. Commission's opinion and order, May 17, 1971, requiring divestiture and 10-year prohibition of acquisitions in the cabinet hardware field. Court of Appeals (CA-2) affirmed No. 21, 1972; certiorari denied June 4, 1973. Divestiture accomplished, 1975."[9]

A rate of ten per cent was used to discount the benefits accruing in the years following the date a case was filed. This measure exceeds the rate of return on most investments in the economy during most of the sample period. The reason for a relatively high discount rate is to incorporate the high uncertainty about future benefits. If, for example, a technological innovation occurred several years following the filing date, the subsequent change in industry structure could nullify all future benefits. The relatively high discount rate incorporates this degree of uncertainty.

Based on equation 6-1, the net direct redistribution benefits for the seventy cases between 1954 and 1974 for which data was available are listed in table 6-1. Not all of the cases contributed wealth redistribution benefits. Some cases, as explained previously, did not achieve effective relief. There were eleven cases in which there was no effective remedy. Similarly, other cases were assigned zero direct benefits because they involved a merger that did not increase the four-firm concentration ratio. There were seven cases with zero direct benefits because the merger presumably had no effect on the price-cost margin in the relevant market.

Based on all seventy cases in table 6-1, the average net direct redistribution benefit is $12.70 million per case. Excluding those cases not obtaining effective relief raises the average to $15.06 million of direct benefits per case. If only those cases attaining some positive level of benefits are included, each case contributed an average of $17.09 million.

Table 6-1.   Direct Benefits from Wealth Redistribution (in millions of dollars)

Date of Complaint	Company Challenged	Case Number	Direct Benefits (Bqd)	
1954	Crown Zellerbach Corp.	D6180-DJ	.41	
1955	Schenley Industries,Inc.	C1686-DJ	0.00	***
1955	General Shoe Corporation	C20001-DJ	0.00	***
1955	Union Bag and Paper Corporation	D63801-FTC	16.20	
1955	A.G. Spalding and Brothers, Inc.	D6478-FTC	3.41	
1956	Scovill Manufacturing	D6527-FTC	0.00	***
1956	Vendo Company	D6646-FTC	0.00	***
1956	Gulf Oil Corporation	D6689-FTC	0.00	***
1956	American Radiator and Standard	C14469-DJ	24.23	
1957	National Sugar Refinery Company	D6852-FTC	20.52	
1958	National Alfalfa Dehy- drating and Milling Co.	C6111-DJ	1.15	
1958	Anheuser-Busch	C8906-DJ	4.69	
1959	Diebold, Inc.	C4485-DJ	0.00	****
1959	National Homes	C114-DJ	15.26	
1960	Simpson Timber Company	D7113-FTC	10.56	
1960	Continental Baking	D7880-FTC	21.80	
1961	Koppers Co., Inc.	C6113-DJ	1.28	
1961	Kaiser Aluminum and Chemical Corp.	C61C148DJ	11.72	
1962	Richfield Oil	C621374-DJ	0.00	**
1963	Ingersoll-Rand Company	C63-124-DJ	15.59	
1963	High Voltage Engineering Corp.	C322-FTC	.87	
1963	Diamond Alkali Company	D8572-FTC	3.13	
1963	Frito-Lay	D8606-FTC	25.09	
1964	American Brake Shoe Co.	D8612-FTC	4.85	
1964	Georgia Pacific Corp.	C751-FTC	0.00	***
1964	Joseph Schlitz Brewing Company	C42127-DJ	57.68	

Table 6-1 (Continued)

Date of Complaint	Company Challenged	Case Number	Direct Benefits (Bqd)	
1964	Crown Textile Manufacturing Co., Inc.	C35420-DJ	3.17	
1964	Monsanto Company	C64342-DJ	20.71	
1964	American Pipe and Construction Co.	C641775-DJ	1.95	
1965	Hat Corp. of America	C10980-DJ	.61	
1965	Russell Stover Candies, Inc.	C11474-DJ	13.65	
1965	Penzoil Company	C65838-DJ	33.21	
1965	Heff Jones	C38980-DJ	.79	
1965	Pittsburg Brewing Co.	C651406-DJ	0.00	**
1965	Dean Foods Company	D8674-FTC	37.91	
1966	Schlenley Industries, Inc.	C66-DJ	6.41	
1966	Reed Roller B. & Co.	C66248-DJ	1.82	
1967	Eversharp Inc.	C43623-DJ	68.16	
1967	Cooper Industries, Inc.	C67360-DJ	0.00	**
1967	Simmonds Precision Products, Inc.	C4506-DJ	.65	
1967	Foremost Dairies, Inc.	C1161-FTC	30.10	
1967	Bendix Corporation	D8739-FTC	12.89	
1967	Rexall Drug and Chemical Co.	C1252-FTC	49.95	
1968	Swingline, Inc.	D8759-FTC.	4.54	
1968	Stanley Works	D8760-FTC	6.34	
1968	Vulcan Materials Company	C1409-FTC	0.00	**
1968	Occidental Petroleum	C1450-FTC	37.76	
1968	Work Wear Corporation	C68467	0.00	**
1968	Diamond International Corp.	C5051-DJ	24.75	
1969	Burlington Industries, Inc.	C1473-FTC	0.00	***
1969	Avnet Inc.	D8775-FTC	5.25	
1969	Papercraft Corporation	D8779-FTC	8.30	
1969	Litton Industries, Inc.	D8778-FTC	0.00	***
1969	Chemetron Corporation	D1567-FTC	0.00	***
1969	Iowa Beef Packers, Inc.	C69C-DJ	24.74	
1970	P.R. Mallory and Company, Inc.	C34893-DJ	3.00	
1970	Combustion Engineering, Inc.	C1399-DJ	6.92	
1970	Occidental Petroleum Corporation	C1749-FTC	0.00	***
1971	North American Rockwell Corporation	D8842-FTC	23.60	
1971	St. Joe Mineral Corp.	D8892-FTC	19.20	
1971	Legget and Platt, Inc.	C7976-DJ	1.85	
1972	United Foam Corporation	C1490-DJ	2.62	
1972	Converse Rubber Corp.	722075-DJ	20.49	
1972	Marathon Enterprises, Incorporated	C197872-DJ	2.03	

Table 6-1 (continued)

Date of Complaint	Company Challenged	Case Number	Direct Benefits (Bqd)
1973	Guardian Industries	C73383-DJ	0.00 **
1973	American Technical Industries, Inc.	C73246	1.20
1973	Goodyear Tire and Rubber Company	C73835-DJ	40.87
1973	Firestone Tire and Rubber Company	C73836-DJ	21.79
1973	Leggett and Myer Inc.	D8938-FTC	12.11
1974	Walter Kiddie and Company	D8957-FTC	0.00 ***
1974	Legget and Platt, Inc.	C74CV18-DJ	.83

    ** Merger did not increase four-firm concentration ratio.
  *** Merger did not obtain any relief.
**** Both of the above.

It is clear from table 6-1 that the speed within which effective relief is achieved is a major determinant of the magnitude of the direct benefits. Table 6-2 shows the flow of annual discounted benefits over the first six periods following the case-filing date for a selected sample of cases. It is apparent that in the cases where relief is obtained in a period shortly after the case was initiated, the benefits are higher relative to VS_a. That is, as n^*-n becomes smaller, B_{qd}/VS_a becomes larger, for any given case. In *Rexall Drug*, $B_{qd}/VS_a = .68$ and $n^*-n = 1$. This is a contrast to the case against *Spalding*, where $B_{qd}/VS_a = .31$ and $n^*-n = 8$. Thus, the magnitude of B_{qd} varies directly with the speed of relief.

The Deterrent Effect

As previously noted, many researchers have recognized the importance of deterrence as a benefit of antitrust policy. In chapter 4 it was estimated that each horizontal merger case prevented an average of between nine and fourteen large horizontal mergers from occurring. Had these acquisitions taken place, according to equation 6-1, there would have been a redistribution of wealth from consumers to firms. Thus, benefits of the type measured by equation 6-1 are obtained from the deterrent effect.

    Because of the different models used to predict merger activity, chapter 4 concluded with seven estimates of average deterrence. To test the sensitivity of the redistribution benefits to the magnitude of the deterrent effect, three measures of average deterrence are used throughout this chapter: (1) the largest estimate, 13.76 mergers deterred per case; (2) the smallest estimate, 8.98 mergers deterred per case; and (3) the average of

Table 6-2.   Annual Discounted Direct Redistribution for Selected Cases (millions of dollars)

		Rexall Drug	Spalding	National Alfalfa	Reed Roller
	VS_a	74.00	11.00	3.70	2.70
Years Following Case Filing	0	0.00	0.00	0.00	0.00
	1	5.01	0.00	0.00	0.18
	2	4.58	0.00	0.00	0.17
	3	4.17	0.00	0.00	0.15
	4	3.79	0.00	0.19	0.14
	5	3.45	0.00	0.17	0.13
	6	3 13	0.00	0.16	0.11
		.	.	.	.
		.	.	.	.
		.	.	.	.
	Total	49.95	11.00	3.70	1.82

all seven estimates, 10.58 mergers deterred per case. The "average" average deterrent measure will be used most frequently and compared with the upper and lower estimates to test for the robustness of the results.

Although a case may occur in a given period, i, it is not likely that all of the deterred mergers would have occurred in that same period. That is, if average deterrence, $\overline{MD}$, is 10.58, not all of the 10.58 mergers would have taken place at the same time. What is the structure of deterrence over periods i+1, i+2, . . . , i+k? And what is the percentage of $\overline{MD}$ occurring in each period i, i+1, . . . , i+k? Does a greater amount of deterrence occur in the beginning or later periods after a case has been filed? Answers to these questions can be inferred from the empirical results in chapter 4.

In the models predicting merger activity, the variable representing antitrust policy was a cumulative index of merger enforcement relative to merger activity. It was found that including either the previous four or six years in the index yielded the highest t-ratios. Since the index was lagged one year behind the dependent variable, merger activity, it follows that merger cases affect merger activity for the following six years. That is, given a case in period i, according to the empirical results in chapter 4 the deterred mergers would have taken place in periods i+1, i+2, . . . , i+6.

Two methods were found to be successful in weighting the years included in the cumulative index of relative merger enforcement: (1) equal weights for each year, and (2) weighting the more recent years more heavily. These weights provide a basis for an analogous distribution for the deterrent effect.

The structure of deterrence, $\overline{MD}$, over k periods is therefore

$$\overline{MD} = \sum_{i=1}^{k} w_i \cdot \overline{MD}$$

where $\sum_{i=1}^{k} w_i = 1$, and w_i is the selected weight in period i. Using equal weights for each year results in

$$w_i = 1/k, \qquad \text{for } i = 1, \ldots, k.$$

If, as discussed previously, k=6, then $w_1 = w_2 = \ldots = w_6 = .1667$. Given $\overline{MD} = 10.58$,

$$\overline{MD}_i = w_i \cdot \overline{MD}, \qquad \text{for } i = 1, \ldots, k$$

or $\overline{MD}_i = 1.76$. Thus, for a structure of deterrence equally weighted over the six years immediately following a case, 1.76 mergers are deterred in each year.

Using the structure of decreasing weights over a six-year period, $w_i, = .7^i$, and given $\overline{MD} = 10.58$, yields the following:

$w_1 = .340$	$\overline{MD}_1 = 3.60$
$w_2 = .238$	$\overline{MD}_2 = 2.52$
$w_3 = .167$	$\overline{MD}_3 = 1.80$
$w_4 = .117$	$\overline{MD}_4 = 1.24$
$w_5 = .082$	$\overline{MD}_5 = .86$
$w_6 = .057$	$\overline{MD}_6 = .60$

The structure with declining weights has the desirable property of a gradually decaying deterrent effect. This is especially desirable when compared to the constant weighting schemes where an identical number of mergers are deterred for k years following a case, but in period k+1, and all subsequent years, deterrence is zero. It seems more intuitively plausible that deterrence should decrease gradually, rather than drastically through a quantum change. Thus, decreasing weights will be used throughout the remainder of this chapter to estimate the structure of deterrence.

The deterrent effect has been referred to previously in terms of numbers of cases. However, the benefits measured by equation 6-1 are in terms of dollars, based on the value of shipments of the acquired firm. What would the size of the deterred mergers have been had these acquisitions occurred? The most likely candidate to represent the size of mergers that never took place because of antitrust enforcement is the size of the acquired firm in the case. In his paper, discussed in chapter 2, Weiss assumes that the deterrent effect of a case is proportional to the sales of the acquired firm. He explains, "This assumption seems roughly plausible because publicity for ordinary enforcement cases (as opposed to test cases) is probably roughly proportional to the size of the case."[10] That is, deterrence occurs when firms are aware of the enforcement of the law and modify their behavior accordingly. When larger firms are involved in a case, attention is more likely to be focused on the vigor of the antitrust agencies, resulting in a larger deterrent effect.

Using the value of shipments in a merger case to approximate the size of the deterred mergers, the net indirect welfare redistribution benefits, B_{qi}, can be measured by

$$B_{qi} = \sum_{n=1}^{N} \frac{\sum_{i=1}^{6} (w_i \cdot DVS_a)}{(1 + d)^n} \cdot (1 - tr) \cdot b \qquad (6\text{-}2)$$

where the size of the deterred merger, DVS_a, is formed from

$$DVs_a = \overline{MD_i} \cdot VS_a$$

and is weighted by the structure discussed above.

Table 6-3 lists the net indirect benefits using three measures of average deterrence. Unlike the direct gain, all cases contribute a positive amount of benefits resulting from deterrence. This is because the direct benefits are conditional upon effective relief and the effect the merger has on the four-firm concentration ratio, while the indirect benefits are based solely on the size of the acquired firm.

Table 6-3. Indirect Benefits from Wealth Redistribution (millions of dollars)

Company Challenged	Bqi for MD=10.58	Bqi for MD=13.76	Bqi for MD=8.98
Crown Zellerbach Corporation	9.36	12.17	7.95
Schlenley Industries, Inc.	109.62	142.51	93.06
General Shoe Corporation	369.08	479.80	313.31
Union Bag and Paper Corp.	132.21	171.87	112.23
A.G Spalding and Bros., Inc.	60.59	78.77	51.43
Scovill Manufacturing	4.41	5.73	3.74
Vendo Company	38.56	50.13	32.73
Gulf Oil Corporation	550.88	716.14	467.85
American Radiator and Standard	273.23	355.20	231.94
National Sugar Refining Co.	231.37	300.78	196.41
National Alfalfa Dehydrating Company	20.38	26.49	17.30
Anheuser-Busch	47.38	61.59	40.22
Diebold	55.09	71.62	46.77
National Homes	154.25	200.53	130.94
Simpson Timber Company	211.54	275.00	179.58
Continental Baking	220.35	286.46	187.06
Koppers Company, Inc.	10.47	13.61	8.89
Kaiser Aluminum and Chemical Corporation	132.21	171.87	112.23
Richfield Oil	511.72	665.24	434.40
Ingersoll-Rand Company	127.25	165.43	108.02
High Voltage Engineering Company	13.77	17.90	11.70
Diamond Alkali	35.26	45.84	29.93
Frito-Lay, Incorporated	396.63	515.62	336.70
American Brake Shoe Company	68.31	88.80	57.99
Georgia Pacific Corporation	271.03	352.34	230.08
Joseph Schlitz Brewing Co.	423.62	550.71	359.61
Crown Textile Manufacturing Company	25.89	33.66	21.98
Monsanto Company	209.33	272.13	177.70
American Pipe and and Construction	27.54	35.80	23.38
Hat Corporation of America	5.51	7.16	4.68
Russell Stover Candies, Inc.	123.95	161.14	105.22
Penzoil Company	271.03	352.34	230.08
Heff Jones	7.16	9.31	6.08
Pittsburg Brewing Company	163.61	212.70	138.90
Dean Foods Company	427.48	555.72	362.89
Schlenley Industries, Inc.	90.34	117.44	76.69

Table 6-3 (continued)

Company Challenged	Bqi for MD=10.58	Bqi for MD=13.76	Bqi for MD=8.98
Reed Roller Bit Company	14.87	19.33	12.62
Eversharp, Inc.	688.59	895.17	584.54
Cooper Industries, Inc.	33.05	42.97	28.06
Simmonds Precision Products, Incorporated	6.61	8.60	5.61
Foremost Dairies, Inc.	245.69	319.40	208.57
Bendix Corporation	203.82	264.97	173.02
Rexall Drug and Chemical Co.	407.65	529.95	346.05
Swingline Incorporated	51.23	66.60	43.49
Stanley Works	100.26	130.34	85.11
Vulcan Materials Company	30.30	39.39	25.72
Occidental Petroleum	381.16	495.51	323.57
Workwear Corporation	19.28	25.06	16.37
Diamond International Corp.	181.79	236.33	154.32
Burlington Industries, Inc.	372.94	484.82	316.59
Avnet Incorporated	66.11	85.94	56.12
Papercraft Corporation	93.65	121.75	79.49
Litton Industries, Inc.	286.45	372.39	243.17
Chemetron Corporation	137.72	179.04	116.91
Iowa Beef Packers, Inc.	391.12	508.46	332.02
P.R. Mallory and Co., Inc.	22.04	28.65	18.71
Combustion Engineering, Inc.	69.96	90.95	59.39
Occidental Petroleum Corp.	512.84	666.69	435.35
North American Rockwell Corporation	266.07	345.89	225.87
St. Joe Mineral Corporation	141.02	183.33	119.71
Legget and Platt, Inc.	29.20	37.96	24.79
United Foam Corporation	33.05	42.97	28.06
Converse Rubber Corporation	264.42	343.74	224.47
Marathon Enterprises, Inc.	14.87	19.33	12.62
GuardianIndustries	3.31	4.30	2.81
American Technical Industries	8.81	11.45	7.48
Goodyear Tire and Rubber Co.	413.46	537.76	351.16
Firestone Tire & Rubber Co.	220.35	286.46	187.06
Legget and Myers Inc.	152.59	198.37	129.53
Walter Kiddie and Company	26.44	34.37	22.44
Legget and Platt, Inc.	10.47	13.61	8.89

Total net benefits from the redistribution of wealth are obtained by summing the direct and indirect benefits,

$$B_q = B_{qd} + B_{qi}$$

Using the average cost estimates from chapter 5, the benefit-cost ratios, based on the total redistribution gain, were calculated and are listed in table 6-4.

It should be remembered that, even though the primary motivation behind the antitrust laws appears to be the distributive effect, a dollar redistributed is not strictly comparable with a dollar of public expenditure. That is, the benefits measured by B_q do not represent an increase in national output; the country is not wealthier, in terms of total goods and services, because of the redistribution of wealth. There has been no net increase in production resulting from this redistribution.

A useful interpretation of the benefit-cost ratios in table 6-4 is that they indicate the amount of redistribution benefits accruing from each dollar spent on the case. This provides a guideline for decision-makers who must choose a standard for the minimum amount of wealth redistributed from one dollar's worth of enforcement for the case to be economically efficient. For example, suppose that the subjective weight for one dollar of redistributed wealth, α, is five per cent. Such a criterion implies that of each dollar of benefits, only five cents represents a gain in social welfare. Thus, for each dollar expended, there must be twenty dollars, or $1/\alpha$, redistributed for the case to be economically efficient. Any case with redistribution benefits less than twenty times the cost incurred in undertaking that case represents a waste of public resources.

Table 6-4. Benefit-Cost Ratios from Wealth Redistribution

Company Challenged	B_q/AC for MD=10.58	B_q/AC for MD=13.76	B_q/AC for MD=8.98
Crown Zellerbach Corp.	6.56	8.53	5.57
Schlenley Industries, Inc.	72.12	93.56	61.22
General Shoe Corporation	242.82	315.67	206.13
Union Bag and Paper Corp.	97.64	126.93	82.89
A.G. Spalding and Brothers, Inc.	42.11	54.74	35.75
Scovill Manufacturing	2.81	3.65	2.39
Vendo Company	24.56	31.93	20.85
Gulf Oil Corporation	350.88	456.14	297.86
American Radiator and Standard	189.46	246.30	160.83
National Sugar Refining Co.	155.49	202.14	132.00
National Alfalfa Dehydrating Company	13.05	16.97	11.08
Anheuser-Busch	31.56	41.03	26.79
Diebold, Inc.	32.79	42.63	27.84
National Homes	102.73	133.55	87.21
Simpson Timber Company	132.20	171.86	112.22

Table 6-4 (continued)

Company Challenged	Bq/AC for MD=10.58	Bq/AC for MD=13.76	Bq/AC for MD=8.98
Continental Baking	141.61	184.09	120.21
Koppers Co., Inc.	6.87	8.93	5.83
Kaiser Aluminum Chemical	84.17	109.42	71.45
Richfield Oil	293.59	381.67	249.23
Ingersoll-Rand	80.25	104.33	68.12
High Voltage Engineering Corporation	8.22	10.69	6.98
Diamond Alkali Company	21.57	28.04	18.31
Frito-Lay, Inc.	236.92	308.00	201.12
American Brake Shoe Company	40.42	52.55	34.31
Georgia Pacific Corporation	149.74	194.66	127.11
Joseph Schlitz Brewing Co.	265.91	345.68	225.73
Crown Textile Manufacturing Company	16.06	20.88	13.63
Monsanto Company	127.09	165.22	107.89
American Pipe and Construction	16.29	21.18	13.83
Hat Corporation of America	3.31	4.30	2.81
Russell Stover Candies, Inc.	10.36	13.47	8.79
Penzoil Company	164.45	213.79	139.60
Heff Jones	4.30	5.59	3.65
Pittsburg Brewing Company	91.90	119.47	78.00
Dean Foods Company	251.56	327.03	213.55
Schlenley Industries, Inc.	50.65	65.85	43.00
Reed Roller Bit Co.	8.74	11.36	7.42
Eversharp Incorporated	384.14	499.38	326.10
Cooper Industries, Inc.	1.55	2.02	1.32
Foremost Dairies, Inc.	139.99	181.99	118.84
Bendix Corporation	110.01	143.01	93.39
Rexall Drug and Chemical Co.	232.28	301.96	197.18
Swingline Incorporated	27.07	35.19	22.98
Stanley Works	51.75	67.28	43.93
Vulcan Materials Company	14.71	19.12	12.49
Occidental Petroleum	203.36	264.37	172.63
Work Wear Corporation	9.36	12.17	7.95
Diamond International Corp.	100.26	130.34	85.11
Burlington Industries, Inc.	172.66	224.46	146.57
Avnet Incorporated	33.04	62.95	28.05
Papercraft Corporation	47.20	61.36	40.07

Table 6-4 (continued

Company Challenged	Bg/AC for MD=10.58	Bg/AC for MD=13.76	Bg/AC for MD=8.98
Litton Industries, Inc.	132.62	172.41	112.58
Chemetron Corporation	63.76	82.89	54.13
Iowa Beef Packers, Inc.	192.53	250.29	163.44
P.R. Mallory and Company, Inc.	10.98	14.27	9.32
Combustion Engineering, Inc.	32.17	41.82	27.31
Occidental Petroleum Corp.	224.93	292.41	190.94
North American Rockwell Corporation	121.20	157.56	102.89
St. Joe Mineral Corporation	67.04	87.15	56.91
Legget and Platt, Inc.	13.62	17.71	11.56
United Foam Corporation	14.33	18.63	12.12
Converse Rubber Corporation	114.62	149.01	97.30
Marathon Enterprises, Inc.	6.74	8.82	5.77
Guardian Industries	2.02	2.63	1.75
American Technical Industries	3.79	4.93	3.22
Goodyear Tire and Rubber Co.	171.98	223.57	145.99
Firestone Tire & Rubber Co.	91.72	119.24	77.86
Ligget and Myers Inc.	62.39	81.11	52.96
Walter Kiddie and Company	9.14	11.88	7.76
Legget and Platt, Inc.	3.91	5.08	3.32

Using $\overline{MD}$ = 10.54, the average benefit-cost ratio in table 6-4 is 94.7. That is, for all of the horizontal merger cases evaluated, there is an average of about ninety-five dollars redistributed for every dollar expended on antitrust. However, as can be seen by comparing tables 6-1 and 6-3, the majority of the ninety-five dollars is in the form of prevention, as a result of the deterrent effect.

The distribution of benefit-cost ratios over a wide range is shown in table 6-5. This summary information facilitates some evaluation of the economic efficiency of horizontal merger enforcement. For example, if the subjective weighted value of one dollar redistributed, α, is ten per cent, then about one-fifth (21.4%) of the cases filed were an undesirable use of government resources, on the sole basis of redistribution benefits. If $\alpha = 2\%$, then almost one-half (45.7%) of the cases were inefficient. If $\alpha = 1\%$ then all of the cases represent an economically desirable public investment.

The benefit-cost ratios listed in table 6-5 are based on measures of average deterrence—the total amount of deterrence resulting from the

Table 6-5.   The Size Distribution of Benefit-Cost Ratios, for 70 Cases**

Benefit-Cost Ratios	Number of Cases	Percentage
1-10	15	21.4
11-50	17	24.3
51-100	12	17.1
101-150	10	14.3
151-200	6	8.6
201-250	4	5.7
251-300	4	5.7
300-400	2	2.9
Total	70	100.0

**for $\overline{MD}$-10.58

Celler-Kefauver Act and its subsequent enforcement, allocated equally among enforcement cases. It is also useful to evaluate antitrust policy on a marginal basis. Marginal deterrence measures the addition to total deterrence from undertaking one extra case, given the historical record of merger enforcement.

The amount of deterrence contributed from the marginal case undertaken in each year was estimated in chapter 4 and is shown in table 4-9. Since the identity of the marginal case in each year is known only to administrators responsible for planning at the antitrust agencies, the average of VS_a from all of the cases filed in each year was used to represent the size of the marginal case. That is,

$$VS_a' = \sum_{q=1}^{Q} VS_{a_q} / Q$$

where VS_a' is the value of shipments assigned to the marginal case, and Q is the number of cases in that year.

Substituting VS_a' for VS_a in equations 6-1 and 6-2 enabled estimates of the marginal redistribution benefits in each year. Of course, the gain from an added case to the existing bundle of enforcement activity should be compared to the cost of undertaking that additional case—the marginal cost. Using the estimates of marginal cost from table 5-12 in chapter 5, the benefits can be compared with the cost of undertaking the marginal case in each year. This is shown in table 6-6. The third column indicates the average benefit-cost ratio for each year, based on table 6-4. The fourth column lists the benefit-cost ratio for the marginal case. Because marginal deterrence could not be calculated after 1970, the benefit-cost ratio for the marginal case could not be calculated after 1970.

Table 6-6. Benefit-Cost Ratios for Marginal Case Undertaken in Each Year

Year	Number of Cases	For Redistribution Gain Average Benefit-Cost Ratio for Year**	Benefit-Cost Ratio for Marginal Case***
1954	1	6.56	-
1955	4	113.67	-
1956	4	141.92	105.40
1957	1	155.49	51.09
1958	2	44.61	19.98
1959	2	67.76	31.87
1960	2	136.91	71.79
1961	2	45.52	16.39
1962	1	293.59	106.37
1963	4	86.75	48.60
1964	6	102.59	54.25
1965	6	87.64	37.47
1966	2	29.70	10.83
1967	5	173.59	86.81
1968	6	67.75	26.99
1969	6	106.97	36.11
1970	3	89.36	27.55
1971	3	67.29	-
1972	3	45.25	-
1973	5	66.38	-
1974	2	6.53	-

**for $\overline{MD}=10.58$
***Based on data from Tables 5-12 and 4-8

From table 6-6 two generalizations can be made. First, the benefit-cost ratios are higher using average deterrence rather than marginal deterrence. This makes intuitive sense, because the deterrent effect from precedent cases is included in the average measure, but not in the marginal measure. Also the percentage difference between marginal and average cost of enforcement is not as large as the percentage difference between marginal and average deterrence. Thus, in every year, the benefit-cost ratio using average deterrence exceeds the benefit-cost ratio using marginal deterrence.

The second generalization from table 6-6 is that there appears to be a slight trend of decreasing benefit-cost ratios over time. Clearly, such a trend, if it exists, is not at all definite; there is no smooth functional relationship between time and the benefit-cost ratios.

Allocative Efficiency

By preventing an increase in concentration and a subsequent rise in the price-cost margin, horizontal merger cases also provide benefits in the form of improving allocative efficiency. Unlike the redistribution benefits, which must be subjectively weighted to make judgments about their social value, prevention of the deadweight loss represents pure economic gain. That is, one dollar of benefits in allocative efficiency represents one additional dollar to society's production of real goods and services. Thus, allocative efficiency benefits are unequivocally identical to social welfare benefits.

In chapter 3 the net direct benefit from improvement in allocative efficiency, B_{fd}, resulting from antitrust policy, was derived as

$$B_{fd} = \sum_{n=0}^{N} \frac{.5 \cdot b^2 \cdot (VS_a/VS) \cdot VS_a \cdot \eta \cdot V_n}{(1 + d)^n} \tag{6-3}$$

where VS_a is the value of shipments of the acquired firm, VS is the total value of shipments in the relevant market, b is .144 and η, the elasticity of demand, is assigned a value of one. As in equation 6-1, $V_n = 0$ for $n^* > n$, and $V_n = 1$ for $n^* \leq n$.

To measure the industry value of shipments, the relevant market had to be identified. This was accomplished by referring to the *Merger Case Digest*, which indicates the relevant line of commerce and sections of the country involved in the merger, as determined by the court. The magnitude of VS was identified by adding the *Celler-Kefauver Act: The First 27 Years*, and the *Special Report Series: Concentration Ratios in Manufacturing*, as reference sources.

For example, in the Antitrust Division's case against *Simmonds Precision Products, Inc.* (C4506), the product market is defined very narrowly, as fuel gauging systems for aircraft, helicopters, missiles, and spacecraft. The *Merger Case Digest* reports that, "Liquidometer was also a major producer of fuel gauging systems for aircraft and helicopters, accounting for approximately twenty-six per cent of all sales of such systems during 1964 and 1965. Liquidometer was also one of the major suppliers of such systems for missiles and spacecraft to the United States space system. Its 1964 sales of these systems and related equipment were in excess of $1.2 million."[12] Since the share of the relevant market held by the acquired firm, Liquidometer, was identified along with its sales in the market, it was possible to measure the total market value of shipments.

In other cases the market is defined along broader product lines. For example, in the Commission's complaint against *North American Rockwell Corp.* (D8842), the product market is defined as manufacturing of machines used in manufacturing fabric from yarn, and the geographic market is the United States as a whole. Therefore, the relevant market is the four-digit SIC industry "textile machinery," SIC code 3552, and the size of the market is identified from the Census of Manufacturing.

Accurate information indicating the total value of shipments in the relevant market was obtained for fifty-nine cases. Using these data in equation 6-3 enabled the measurement of the net direct allocative efficiency benefits listed in table 6-7. Comparison with table 6-1 shows that the direct allocative efficiency benefits are considerably less than the redistributive benefits. In fact, in none of the cases do the direct allocative efficiency benefits exceed the average cost of enforcement. If benefit-cost ratios were formed solely on the basis of B_{fd}, in none of the cases would the ratio exceed unity. That is, $(B_{fd}/AC) < 1$, for all cases.

Table 6-7.   Net Direct and Indirect Allocative Efficiency Benefits (millions of dollars)

Company Challenged	B_{fd}	B_{fi} for MD=10.58	B_{fi} for MD=13.76	B_{fi} for MD=8.98
Crown Zellerbach Corp.	.0063	.1422	.1849	.1207
Schlenley Industries, Incorporated	0	.1189	.2456	.1604
General Shoe Corp.	0	1.8135	2.3576	1.5394
Union Bag and Paper Corp.	.0209	.1891	.2458	.1605
A.G. Spalding and Bros., Inc.	.0592	.7397	.9616	.6279
Vendo Company	0	1.0065	1.3085	.8544
Gulf Oil Corp.	0	.5877	.7640	.4989

Table 6-7 (continued)

Company Challenged	B_{fd}	B_{fi} for MD=10.58	B_{fi} for MD=13.76	B_{fi} for MD=8.98
American Radiator and Standard	.2725	2.9825	3.8773	2.5318
National Sugar Refining Company	.1072	1.9152	2.4898	1.6758
National Alfalfa Dehydrating Company	.0108	.1907	.2479	.1619
Anheuser-Busch	.0780	.7869	1.0230	.6680
Diebold, Inc.	0	1.3263	1.7242	1.1259
National Homes	.2680	2.7084	3.5209	2.2992
Simpson Timber Co.	0	1.3425	1.7605	1.1496
Continental Baking	.0325	1.4567	1.8937	1.2366
Koppers Co., Inc.	.0089	.0836	.1087	.0710
Kaiser Aluminum	.0198	.2234	.2904	.1896
Ingersoll-Rand	.0906	.7382	.9600	.6267
High Voltage Engineering	.0176	.2778	.3611	.2358
Diamond Alkali Co.	.0649	.7295	.9484	.6193
Frito-Lay, Inc.	.2171	3.4256	4.4533	2.9080
American Brake Shoe Company	.3076	4.3281	5.6265	3.6741
Joseph Schlitz Brewing Company	.1481	1.0856	1.4113	.9216
Monsanto Company	.2244	2.2647	2.9441	1.9225
American Pipe and Construction	.0432	.6080	.7904	.5161
Hat Corporation of America	.0017	.0150	.0195	.0127
Russell Stover Candies, Inc.	.1246	1.1286	1.4672	.9581
Penzoil Company	.1377	1.1218	1.4583	.9523
Heff Jones	.0028	.0257	.0334	.0218
Dean Foods Company	.0992	1.1162	1.4511	.9475
Schenley Industries, Inc.	.0133	.1875	.2438	.1592
Reed Bit Company	.0378	.3078	.4001	.2613
Foremost Dairies, Inc.	.1505	1.2258	1.5935	1.0406
Rexall Drug and Chemical Company	.2091	1.7028	2.2136	1.4455
Swingline Inc.	.0314	.3534	4594	.3000
Stanley Works	.1994	3.1468	4.0908	2.6713
Vulcan Materials Co.	0	.0836	.1087	.0710
Occidental Petroleum	.0931	.9399	1.2219	.7929
Diamond International	.7045	5.1637	6.7128	4.3835
Burlington Industries, Inc.	0	.9818	1.2763	.8335
Avnet, Inc.	.0064	.0802	.1043	.0681
Papercraft Corporation	.1951	2.1964	2.8553	1.8645

Table 6-7 (continued)

Company Challenged	B_{fd}	B_{fi} for MD=10.58	B_{fi} for MD=13.76	B_{fi} for MD=8.98
Litton Industries, Inc.	0	3.2358	4.2065	2.7469
Chemetron Corporation	0	1.5113	1.9647	1.2829
Iowa Beef Packers, Inc.	.1710	2.698	3.5074	2.2903
P.R. Mallory and Company, Inc.	.1203	.8818	1.1463	.7486
Combustion Engineering, Inc.	.0823	.8301	1.0791	.7047
Occidental Petroleum Corporation	0	3.5115	4.5650	2.9809
North American Rockwell	.1915	2.1548	2.8012	1.8292
Legget and Platt, Inc.	.0130	.2058	.2675	.1747
United Foam Corporation	.0363	.4560	.5928	.3871
Converse Rubber Corporation	.5657	7.1123	9.2460	6.0376
Marathon Enterprises, Inc.	.0325	.2385	.3094	.2020
American Technical Industries	.0070	.0511	.0664	.0434
Goodyear Tire and Rubber	.2272	2.7970	3.6361	2.3744
Firestone Tire and Rubber	.0482	.4864	.6323	.4129
Ligget and Myers, Inc.	.0330	.4160	.5408	.3531
Walter Kiddie and Company	0	.0603	.0784	.0512
Legget and Platt, Inc.	.0163	.2055	.2672	.1744

Like the redistribution benefits, the major allocative efficiency gain is the result of the deterrent effect. In chapter 3 the net indirect benefit from preventing a deadweight loss because of deterrence, B_{fi}, was derived as

$$B_{fi} = \sum_{n=1}^{N} \frac{.5 \cdot b^2 \cdot \sum_{n=1}^{6} ((w_i \cdot \overline{MD}) \cdot (VS_a)^2/VS) \cdot \eta}{(1 + d)^n} \qquad (6\text{-}4)$$

Using the three different measures of average deterrence, $\overline{MD}$, the net indirect allocative efficiency benefits resulting from deterrence were calculated and are listed in table 6-7. These benefits were then added to the direct gain in each case and divided by the average cost of merger enforcement in the appropriate year to obtain the benefit-cost ratios shown in table 6-8.

Total allocative efficiency benefits exceed the cost in sixteen of the fifty-nine cases, when $\overline{MD}$ = 10.58. This implies that, disregarding all redistribution benefits, twenty-seven per cent of the horizontal merger cases analyzed in table 6-8 represent a net gain to society. In these cases the increase in production resulting from the case exceeds the resources expended.

Table 6-8.   Benefit-Cost Ratios from Gain in Allocative Efficiency

Company Challenged	B_f/AC for $\overline{MD}$=10.58	B_f/AC for $\overline{MD}$=13.76	B_f/AC for $\overline{MD}$=8.98
Crown Zellerbach Corp.	.98	.13	.08
Schlenley Industries, Inc.	.12	.16	.11
General Shoe Corporation	1.19	1.55	1.01
Union Bag and Paper Corp.	.13	.18	.12
A.G. Spalding and Bros., Inc.	.53	.68	.45
Vendo Company	.64	.83	.54
Gulf Oil Corporation	.37	.49	.31
American Radiator and Standard	2.54	3.30	2.15
National Sugar Refining Co.	1.29	1.67	1.09
National Alfalfa Dehydrating Company	.12	.16	.10
Anheuser-Bisch	.52	.68	.44
Diebold Incorporated	.79	1.03	.67
National Homes	1.77	2.30	1.50
Simpson Timber Company	.79	1.02	.67
Continental Baking	.87	1.13	.74
Koppers Co., Inc.	.05	.07	.05
Kaiser Aluminum	.14	.18	.12
Ingersoll-Rand	.47	.61	.40
High Voltage Engineering Co.	.17	.22	.14
Diamond Alkali Company	.45	.59	.38
Frito-Lay Incorporated	2.05	2.67	1.74
American Brake Shoe Company	2.55	3.31	2.16
Joseph Schlitz Brewing Co.	.68	.88	.57
Monsanto	1.38	1.80	1.17
American Pipe and Construction	.36	.47	.31

Table 6-8 (continued)

Company Challenged	B_f/AC for $\overline{MD}=10.58$	B_f/AC for $\overline{MD}=13.76$	B_f/AC for $\overline{MD}=8.98$
Hat Corporation of America	.01	.01	.01
Russell Stover Candies, Inc.	.68	.88	.58
Penzoil Company	.68	.89	.58
Heff Jones	.02	.02	.01
Dean Foods	.66	.85	.56
Schlenley Industries, Inc.	.11	.14	.09
Reed Bit Company	.18	.24	.15
Foremost Dairies, Inc.	.70	.91	.59
Rexall Drug and Chemical Co.	.97	1.26	.82
Swingline Inc.	.19	.24	.16
Stanley Works	1.62	2.11	1.38
Vulcan Materials Company	.04	.05	.03
Occidental Petroleum	.50	.65	.42
Diamond International	2.85	3.70	2.42
Burlington Industries, Inc.	.45	.59	.39
Avnet, Inc.	.04	.05	.03
Papercraft Corporation	1.11	1.44	.94
Litton Industries, Inc.	1.50	1.95	1.27
Chemetron Corporation	.70	.91	.59
Iowa Beef Packers, Inc.	1.33	1.73	1.13
P.R. Mallory and Co., Inc.	.44	.57	.37
Combustion Engineering, Inc.	.40	.52	.34
Occidental Petroleum Corp.	1.47	1.91	1.25
North American Rockwell	.98	1.28	.83
Legget and Platt, Inc.	.09	.12	.08
United Foam Corporation	.20	.26	.17
Converse Rubber Corporation	3.08	4.01	2.62
Marathon Enterprises, Inc.	.11	.14	.09
American Technical Industries	.02	.03	.02
Goodyear Tire and Rubber Co.	1.15	1.49	.97
Firestone Tire & Rubber Co.	.20	.26	.17
Ligget and Myers, Inc.	.17	.22	.14
Walter Kiddie and Company	.02	.03	.02
Legget and Platt, Inc.	.08	.10	.07

The number of economically efficient cases, based solely on the allocative efficiency criterion, is the result of a strong deterrent effect. This can be seen by comparing the magnitude of the direct and indirect benefits in table 6-7. Thus, the major value of these cases is in the form of preventing future deadweight losses.

How sensitive are the benefit-cost ratios to the different estimates of average deterrence? Table 6-9 compares the distribution of benefit-cost ratios, according to size, for the three measures of $\overline{MD}$. There are only five more cases where benefits exceed cost when the upper-bound average deterrence is used instead of 10.58. That is, in only eight per cent of the cases does the inequality $(B_f/AC) > 1$, change sign when substituting $\overline{MD} = 13.76$ for 10.58 in equations 6-3 and 6-4.

Similarly, only three fewer cases registered a benefit-cost ratio greater than unity when the lower-bound estimate of average deterrence was substituted for 10.58. Only in three per cent of the cases does the inequality $(B_f/AC) > 1$ change sign when $\overline{MD} = 8.98$ is used instead of 10.58. From table 6-9 it can be inferred that the results are robust for the different estimates of average deterrence. There is little difference in the number of economically efficient cases undertaken, on the sole basis of allocative efficiency, regardless of which estimate of average deterrence is used.

Table 6-9.   The Size Distribution of Benefit-Cost Ratios for Different Estimates of Average Deterrence

Range of Benefit-Cost Ratios	Average Deterrence		
	10.58	13.76	8.98
.01 - .50	31 (51%)	23 (39%)	32 (54%)
.51 - 1.00	13 (22)	16 (27)	14 (24)
1.01 - 1.50	8 (14)	7 (12)	8 (14)
1.51 - 2.00	2 (5)	6 (10)	1 (2)
2.01 - 2.50	1 (2)	2 (3)	3 (5)
2.51 - 3.00	3 (5)	1 (2)	1 (2)
3.01 - 3.50	1 (2)	2 (3)	0 (0)
3.51 - 4.00	0 (0)	2 (3)	0 (0)
Total	59 (100)	59 (99)	59 (101)

It is possible to compare the marginal benefits with the marginal cost of undertaking the marginal case in each year. As in measuring the redistribution marginal benefits, the average of VS_a from all of the cases undertaken in each year, VS_a', was used to represent the size of the marginal acquisition. After substituting VS_a' for VS_a in equation 6-4, the marginal allocative efficiency benefits from horizontal merger enforcement in each year were calculated. These benefits are compared with the marginal cost in table 6-10. For some years the average benefit-cost ratio based on average deterrence exceeds unity. This is not the case for the ratios based on marginal deterrence—$(B_f'/MC) < 1$ in every year. The reason for this disparity is that the average benefit for a case includes the deterrent effect from precedent cases, but the marginal benefit measures only the deterrence resulting from undertaking that case alone. Since the majority of allocative benefits are based on the indirect gain, the smaller amount of external benefits greatly reduces B_f'/MC for the marginal case. Thus, it is not surprising that, solely in terms of allocative efficiency benefits, in none of the years was the marginal case an economically efficient use of public resources.

An Evaluation of Horizontal Merger Enforcement

In chapter 3 the framework for analyzing the effectiveness of horizontal merger enforcement was identified as

$$\frac{B_f + \alpha \, B_q}{C}$$

where α is the subjective weighted value of one dollar of wealth redistributed, and C represents the measure of costs. The difficulty in evaluating antitrust activity is that the benefits on which Congress and economists place primary importance can not be simply added and compared to the expenditure of resources invested to achieve those benefits.

However, it is possible to indirectly compare the benefits and costs from horizontal merger enforcement. Table 6-11 lists the minimum value of α, α^*, that yields a benefit cost ratio of unity. That is, α^* is defined as the value of α such that

$$\frac{B_f + \alpha^* B_q}{C} = 1$$

For all $\alpha > \alpha^*$, the benefits exceed the cost; for all $\alpha < \alpha^*$, the benefits are less than the cost. Thus, α^* is the lower-bound subjective valuation of one dollar redistributed required for the case to be economically efficient.

Table 6-10.   Benefit-Cost Ratios for the Marginal Case Undertaken in Each Year, for Allocative Efficiency Gain

Year	Number of Cases	Average Benefit-Cost Ratio for Year**	Benefit-Cost Ratio for Marginal Case***
1954	1	.10	-
1955	4	.49	-
1956	3	1.18	.88
1957	1	1.29	.42
1958	2	.32	.14
1959	2	1.28	.60
1960	2	.83	.44
1961	2	.10	.03
1962	0	-	-
1963	4	.79	.44
1964	4	1.24	.66
1965	5	.41	.18
1966	2	.15	.05
1967	2	.84	.42
1968	5	1.04	.41
1969	6	.89	.29
1970	3	.77	.24
1971	2	.54	-
1972	3	1.13	-
1973	4	.39	-
1974	2	.05	-

**For $\overline{MD}$=10.58

***Based on data from Tables 5-12 and 4-8

For $\overline{MD}$ = 10.58, α^* varies from 0.00 in those cases where the allocative efficiency benefits exceed the cost, to .2991 in the *Hat Corp. of America* case. This implies that if a policy-maker is willing to spend at least one dollar for $3.34 of wealth redistributed, the *Hat Corp.* case was an economically efficient use of public resources: the social welfare gained as a result of the case exceeded the opportunity cost of the resources invested.

Table 6-12 shows the size distribution of α^* for the different estimates of average deterrence. The results do not vary greatly among the different measures of deterrence. That is, given a level of α, approximately the same number of cases represents an economically efficient use of public

Table 6-11.   Minimum Value of α That Yields a Benefit-Cost Ratio of
              Unity, for Total Net Redistribution and Allocative
              Efficiency Benefits

Company Challenged	for $\overline{MD}$=10.58	for $\overline{MD}$=13.76	for $\overline{MD}$=8.98
Crown Zellerbach Corp.	.1372	.1020	.1652
Schlenley Industries, Inc.	.0122	.0089	.0145
General Shoe Corp.	0	0	0
Union Bag and Paper Corp.	.0089	.0065	.0106
A.G. Spalding and Bros., Inc.	.0112	.0058	.0154
Vendo Company	.0147	.0053	.0221
Gulf Oil Corp.	.0018	.0011	.0023
American Radiator and Standard	0	0	0
National Sugar Refining Co.	0	0	0
National Alfalfa Dehydrating Company	.0574	.0495	.0812
Anheuser-Busch	.0152	.0078	.0209
Diebold Inc.	.0064	0	.0119
National Homes	0	0	0
Simpson Timber Company	.0016	0	.0029
Continental Baking	.0009	0	.0022
Koppers Co., Inc.	.1382	.1041	.1630
Kaiser Aluminum	.0102	.0075	.0123
Ingersoll-Rand	.0066	.0037	.0088
High Voltage Engineering	.1010	.0730	.1232
Diamond Alkali Company	.0255	.0146	.0339
Frito-Lay Inc.	0	0	0
American Brake Shoe Co.	0	0	0
Joseph Schlitz Brewing Co.	.0012	.0004	.0019
Monsanto	0	0	0
American Pipe and Construction	.0393	.0032	.0499
Hat Corporation of America	.2991	.2302	.3523
Russell Stover Candies, Inc.	.0309	.0089	.0478
Penzoil Company	.0019	.0005	.0030
Heff Jones	.2279	.0175	.2712
Dean Foods Company	.0014	.0005	.0021
Schlenley Industries, Inc.	.0176	.0131	.0212
Reed Bit Company	.0938	.0669	.1146
Foremost Dairies, Inc.	.0021	.0005	.0035

Table 6-11 (continued)

Company Challenged	for $\overline{MD}$=10.58	for $\overline{MD}$=13.76	for $\overline{MD}$=8.90
Rexall Drug and Chemical Co.	.0001	0	.0009
Swingline Inc.	.0299	.0216	.0366
Stanley Works	0	0	0
Vulcan Materials Company	.0653	.0497	.0777
Occidental Petroleum	.0025	.0013	.0034
Diamond International	0	0	0
Burlington Industries, Inc.	.0032	.0018	.0042
Avnet Incorporated	.0291	.0013	.0346
Papercraft Corporation	0	0	.0015
Litton Industries, Inc.	0	0	0
Chemetron Corporation	.0047	.0011	.0076
Iowa Beef Packers, Inc.	0	0	0
P.R. Mallory and Co., Inc.	.0510	.0310	.0676
Combustion Engineering, Inc.	.0187	.0115	.0242
Occidental Petroleum Corp.	0	0	0
North American Rockwell	.0002	0	.0017
Legget and Platt, Inc.	.0668	.0497	.0796
United Foam Corporation	.0558	.0397	.0683
Converse Rubber Corporation	0	0	0
Marathon Enterprises, Inc.	.1311	.0974	.1577
American Technical Industries	.2586	.1968	.3043
Goodyear Tire and Rubber	0	0	.002
Firestone Tire and Rubber	.0087	.0062	.0107
Ligget and Myers, Inc.	.0133	.0106	.0157
Walter Kiddie and Company	.1072	.0816	.1263
Legget and Platt, Inc.	.2353	.1772	.2801

resources, regardless of which of the estimates of average deterrence is used. For example, if α is selected as one per cent, then 32 of the cases had net social benefits, given $\overline{MD}$ = 10.58; 39 had net social benefits, given $\overline{MD}$ = 13.76; and 29 had net social benefits when $\overline{MD}$ = 8.98.

Table 6-12 provides a summary evaluation of horizontal merger enforcement. Given a level of α, the number of cases that were economically efficient consists of all the cases for which $\alpha^* < \alpha$. This is shown more clearly in figure 6-1, which is essentially a cumulative density function for the percentage of economically efficient cases for increasing levels of

α^*. Three different functions are shown, each representing a different level of average deterrence. Between twenty-two per cent and thirty-four per cent, depending upon the measure of $\overline{MD}$, of horizontal merger cases represent an unambiguous, economically efficient investment of public resources. Even if redistribution benefits are considered socially worthless, that is $\alpha = 0$, these cases still yielded a net social gain on the basis of their allocative efficiency benefits. Thus, the intercept of the functions in figure 6-1 indicates the percentage of cases that were unequivocally economically efficient.

Table 6-12.   The Size Distribution of α^* for Different Estimates of Average Deterrence[@]

	Average Deterrence		
Range of α^*	10.58	13.76	8.98
0	15 (26%)	20 (34%)	13 (22%)
.0001 – .005	12 (20)	12 (20)	13 (22)
.006 – .010	5 (9)	7 (12)	3 (5)
.011 .050	12 (20)	11 (19)	15 (25)
.051 – .100	6 (10)	4 (7)	5 (9)
.101 – .150	5 (9)	2 (3)	3 (5)
.151 – .200	0 (0)	2 (3)	3 (5)
.201 – .250	2 (3)	1 (2)	0 (0)
.251 – .300	2 (3)	0 (0)	2 (3)
.301 – .400	0 (0)	0 (0)	2 (3)
Total	59 (100)	59 (100)	59 (100)

[@]α^* is the minimum value of α that yields a benefit-cost ratio of one.

As larger levels of α^* are selected, the greater is the number of efficient horizontal merger cases. For $\overline{MD} = 10.55$, forty-six per cent of the cases were efficient for $\alpha^* = .5$ per cent. This means that if $200 of wealth is redistributed for every dollar of expense incurred in an antitrust case, about half of the cases were economically efficient. If $100 of redistribution is required for each dollar spent, eighty-seven per cent of the cases represent a net social gain. If $3.33 of redistribution must occur for a case to be efficient, then all of the horizontal merger cases represented an appropriate use of public resources.

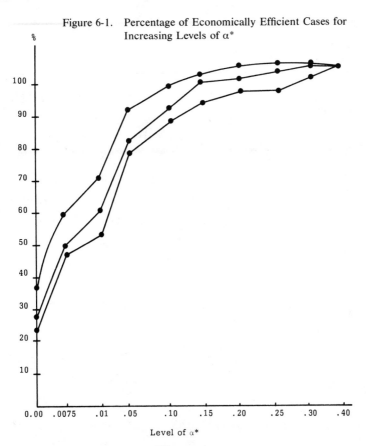

Figure 6-1.   Percentage of Economically Efficient Cases for Increasing Levels of α^*

Upper function represents $\overline{MD}$ = 13.76
Middle function represents $\overline{MD}$ = 10.58
Lower function represents $\overline{MD}$ = 8.98

7

Conclusions

Have the benefits from horizontal merger enforcement justified the costs? Is the Celler-Kefauver Amendment merely a "charade," a futile effort by the antitrust agencies that succeeds only in postponing the inevitable? The purpose of this study was to evaluate horizontal merger enforcement made feasible by the Celler-Kefauver Act and provide some insight into these questions.

In the introductory chapter the goals of antitrust were identified as being multi-dimensional. However, based on apparent Congressional intent, two widely-held social and economic values—the redistribution of wealth from monopoly power to consumers and the improvement of allocative efficiency—emerged as underlying motivations behind the antitrust laws. It should be remembered that this study ignores all other social and political gains associated with antitrust enforcement. There probably exist other benefits, consistent with the purposes of Congress, resulting from antitrust activity. To the degree that these other values can be identified, the findings of this study should be qualified.

Judging the efficiency of the allocation of antitrust resources by the enforcement agencies has been a popular topic in the antitrust literature. Chapter 2 reviewed the most important of these studies and discovered that a common conclusion among researchers is that antitrust resources are not being allocated in a way that greatly enhances social welfare. The general findings of this literature is that the budgets at the Antitrust Division and the FTC are typically spent pursuing per se violations in unconcentrated industries. However, one shortcoming common to all of these papers, with the sole exception of "An Analysis of the Allocation of Antitrust Division Resources" by Leonard Weiss, is that judgments are made about the resource allocation of the enforcement agencies with only partial knowledge of the benefits yielded from cases and virtually no knowledge of the costs of undertaking these cases.

Thus, in chapter 3 a formal framework for measuring the benefits from horizontal merger enforcement and comparing them with the costs was introduced. The contribution of a merger case to wealth redistribution and allocative efficiency is based on a paper by Preston and Collins finding a positive significant linear relationship between the four-firm concentration ratio and the price-cost margin. An implication from this study is that a merger which increases the concentration ratio leads to a subsequent rise in the price-cost margin. Based on the size of the acquired firm the distributive effect of such a merger was algebraically derived. Similarly, the allocative efficiency effect was found to be related to the value of shipments of the acquired firm relative to the size of the market. Therefore, prohibition of an acquisition increasing the four-firm concentration ratio prevents the redistribution of wealth and loss in allocative efficiency.

A horizontal merger case provides not only the direct gains mentioned above, but also provides benefits because subsequent acquisitions and consolidations are deterred. Thus, chapter 4 was an excursion into the counter-factual. In answering the question, "What would horizontal merger activity have been in the absence of Celler-Kefauver enforcement?" the deterrent effect was estimated. Two different methods were used to measure the indirect benefits from a horizontal merger case. The first procedure estimated a model explaining horizontal merger activity over a pre-Celler-Kefauver enforcement period. It was found that a regression for 1919 to 1954 best represented the regime prior to effective enforcement of the amended Section 7. The number of mergers increasing the four-firm concentration ratio that would have occurred in the absence of antitrust enforcement during the ensuing years was predicted by extrapolating from the historical values of the explanatory variables. The residual between predicted and actual merger activity was then attributed to deterrence.

The second method included dummy variables representing precedent cases and an index of cumulative merger enforcement relative to merger activity in a 1919-to-1976 model estimating merger activity. Mergers in the absence of Celler-Kefauver enforcement were predicted by assigning the antitrust variables a value of zero. Deterrence was then measured as the difference between predicted and actual merger activity.

Based on the regression analysis it was found that the estimates of the deterrent effect were not particularly sensitive to either the number of years included in the cumulative index of relative merger enforcement or the weights assigned to each lagged year. Using seven different models, average deterrence per case was found to vary between 8.98 and 13.76, with an average of 10.58. That is, on the average, each case prevented slightly less than eleven large horizontal mergers from occurring.

The structural form selected to represent the cumulative index of relative merger enforcement also enabled an approximation of marginal deterrence. Marginal deterrence with respect to time was defined as the addition to total deterrence from undertaking one extra case, given the historical record of merger enforcement. As might be expected, since this measure excludes the deterrent effect from precedent cases, marginal deterrence for each year was considerably less than average deterrence.

The purpose of chapter 5 was to determine the cost of undertaking a horizontal merger case. Measures approximating both marginal and average cost were estimated. The number of hours expended by the FTC staff on all matters that were closed from July 1974 to May 1978 were obtained from the Office of the Secretary at the FTC. This included all the hours spent by attorneys, economists, staff, and Administrative Law Judges since the inception of the matter.

The cost of undertaking a horizontal merger case consists not only of time spent directly on that case but also resources used searching through many matters to identify feasible cases. Therefore, the time expended on investigations that were opened but subsequently dropped before reaching the litigation or consent stage was also estimated. This was done by assuming a constant flow of agency activity over the case-selection cycle. Under this assumption it could be inferred that the same amount of resources expended in searching for cases during the 1974 to 1977 sample period were spent in earlier years in searching for the cases which were ultimately closed between 1974 and 1977. Since this measure includes only activities spent directly on cases, it approximates marginal cost. The average cost of undertaking a merger case was derived from the proportion of the antitrust agencies' budgets devoted to merger enforcement, divided by the number of cases. This measure exceeded the marginal cost because it included administrative and other overhead expenses.

Inspection of the number of hours spent on each case revealed a wide variance of costs, casting some doubt about the applicability of assigning a constant cost to all cases outside of the sample. However, from unsuccessful regressions trying to explain the number of hours spent on a case based on several firm attributes, it was deduced that the cost of a case cannot be predicted, a priori, by firm characteristics. This somewhat justified applying the derived measures of cost on a per case basis.

This study contributed no new information about private expenditures in horizontal merger cases. Therefore, the approximation of private costs used in Weiss's paper was adapted.

Chapter 6 incorporated the results of all the previous chapters to estimate the benefits from horizontal merger enforcement and make a comparison with the costs, enabling an evaluation of horizontal merger enforcement. Using the methodology from chapter 3, along with the various assumptions about the deterrent effect, lower and upper limits of the redistribution of wealth and allocative efficiency benefits from a sample of horizontal merger cases were estimated. The average net direct redistribution gain for seventy cases was calculated to be $12.70 million per case. It should be remembered that even though the primary motivation behind the antitrust laws was the distributive effect, a dollar redistributed is not strictly comparable with a dollar of public expenditure. Therefore, the social virtue of this redistribution is based on normative standards.

As might be expected, the indirect redistribution benefits resulting from deterrence were considerably larger than the direct gain. This is because the direct benefits were conditional upon effective relief, while the indirect gain was based solely on the size of the acquired firm.

Unlike the redistribution benefits, which must be subjectively weighted to make judgments about their social value, prevention of the deadweight loss represents unqualified economic gain. In none of the cases did the direct allocative efficiency benefit exceed the average cost of a merger case. However, when including the indirect benefits, in fifteen of the cases the allocative efficiency gain exceeded the cost. This suggests that about one-quarter of the cases represented unequivocal net social gains.

From the estimates of the benefit-cost ratios based on the upper and lower bounds for deterrence it was inferred that the results were quite robust with respect to the different measures of deterrence. There was little difference found in the number of economically efficient cases undertaken, regardless of which estimate of average deterrence was used.

The number of economically efficient cases based on total benefits—wealth redistribution plus allocative efficiency—depends upon the normative valuation of a dollar redistributed. That is, for the mean measure of average deterrence, if a policymaker regards $200 redistributed as being equivalent to a one dollar gain in social welfare, about half of the cases were economically efficient. As more value is attached to the distributional effect, the greater is the number of economically efficient cases. If only $100 of redistribution is required for each dollar of public expenditure, then eighty-seven per cent of the cases represented a net social gain.

Based on the intent of Congress, it appears that society considers the distributive effect as a genuine social value. Therefore, although such an equivalence was never explicitly provided by those responsible for enacting the antitrust laws, it does not seem unreasonable to equate one dollar of public expenditures with one hundred dollars of redistribution. Under such a standard, which most likely understates the intent of Congress, almost ninety per cent of the cases represented an economically efficient use of public resources in the sense that their contribution to social welfare exceeded their opportunity cost.

Of course, to the degree that the distribution effect is discounted, the fewer were the number of economically efficient cases. However, even if no value is attached to wealth redistribution, about one-quarter of the cases still represented a net economic gain.

Similarly, if the distributive effect is held in very high esteem, almost all of the cases were economically efficient. If $3.33 of redistribution is equivalent to a one dollar gain in social welfare, then none of the cases examined were a waste of public resources.

It can be concluded, therefore, that the success of horizontal merger enforcement depends upon the valuation of the redistribution effect. If one is at odds with Congressional intent, the number of economically efficient cases that were undertaken could conceivably be as low as twenty-five per cent. However, if even a mild value is placed on the distributive effect, the majority of the cases yielded a net economic gain.

From the results of this study it appears that, based on two of the major social and economic values implicit in the antitrust laws—the redistribution of wealth and allocative efficiency—horizontal merger enforcement has been remarkably successful. Even though many of the cases did not yield a large direct benefit, the deterrent value was a justifiable reason for undertaking the case. Therefore, from the results of this study, it can be concluded that the Celler-Kefauver Act and its subsequent enforcement has enhanced social and economic welfare.

Notes

Chapter 1

1. Harbeson, Robert H. "The Clayton Act: Sleeping Giant of Antitrust?" *American Economic Review,* 1958.

2. Galbraith, John K., *The New Industrial State.* Boston: Houghton Mifflin Co., 1967, pp. 187, 197.

3. Scherer, F. M., "The Posnerian Harvest: Separating Wheat from Chaff," *Yale Law Review* 86, (April 1977): 974-1002, p. 977.

4. Bork, Robert H., "Legislative Intent and the Policy of the Sherman Act," *Journal of Law and Economics,* 60, (October 1966): 7-48, p. 47.

5. Bork, p. 7.

6. Bork, p. 16.

7. Weiss, Leonard W., "An Analysis of the Allocation of Antitrust Division Resources," in James A. Dalton and Stanford L. Levin, editors, *The Antitrust Dilemma.* Lexington: D. C. Heath and Company, 1974, p. 35.

8. Weiss, Leonard W., "The Concentration-Profits Relationship and Antitrust," in Harvey J. Goldschmid, H. Michael Mann, and J. Fred Weston, editors, *Industrial Concentration: The New Learning.* Boston: Little, Brown, and Company, 1974.

9. Mueller, Willard F., *The Celler-Kefauver Act: The First 27 Years,* a staff report to the Subcommittee on Monopolies and Commercial Law, 95th Congress, 2nd session, December, 1978, p. 18.

10. Quoted at Scherer, p. 980.

11. *Northern Securities Company v. United States,* 193 U.S. 197, 1904.

12. *Standard Oil Company v. United States,* 221 U.S. 1, 1911.

13. Nelson, Ralph L., *Merger Movements in American Industry 1895-1956,* National Bureau of Economic Research, General Studies No. 66. Princeton: Princeton University Press, 1959.

14. Stigler, George J., "Monopoly and Oligopoly by Merger," *American Economic Review Papers and Proceedings,* (May 1950), p. 23.

15. Martin, David Dale, *Mergers and the Clayton Act.* Berkeley: University of California Press, 1959, p. 45.

16. Public Law No. 212, 38 U.S. Stat. at L. (1914), 730-40.

17. *Arrow-Hart and Hegeman Electric Company v. FTC,* 291 U.S. 581, 1934.

18. Martin, p. 118.

19. Martin, p. 169.

20. Martin, p. 169.

21. Markham, Jesse W., "Mergers: The Adequacy of the New Section 7," in Almarin Phillips, editor, *Perspectives on Antitrust Policy.* Princeton: Princeton University Press, 1965, pp. 167-68.

22. Martin, p. 235.

23. 64 U.S. Stat. at L. (1950), 1125.

24. Markham, p. 166.

25. Eis, Carl, "The 1919-1930 Merger Movement in American Industry," *Journal of Law and Economics,* 12, no. 2, (October 1969): 267-96, p. 293.

26. Posner, Richard A., *Antitrust Law: An Economic Perspective.* Chicago: University of Chicago Press, 1976, p. 97.

Chapter 2

1. Posner, Richard A., "A Statistical Study of Antitrust Enforcement," *Journal of Law and Economics* 13, No. 2 (October 1970): 355-420.

2. Posner, p. 406.

3. Posner, Richard A., "The Federal Trade Commission," *University of Chicago Law Review* 52 (1969): 47-89, p. 55.

4. Posner, 1970, p. 408.

5. Posner, 1970, p. 419.

6. Long, William F., Richard Schramm and Robert Tollison, "The Economic Determinants of Antitrust Activity," *Journal of Law and Economics* 16, No. 2 (October 1973): 351-64.

7. Harberger, Arnold C., "Monopoly and Resource Allocation," 44 *American Economic Review,* part 2, Paper and Proceedings (May 1954).

8. Kamerschen, David R., "An Estimation of the 'Welfare Loss' from Monopoly in the American Economy," *Western Economic Journal* 4 (1966): 221-37.

9. Schwartzman, David, "The Burden of Monopoly," *Journal of Political Economy* 68 (1960): 627-30.

10. Siegfried, John J., "The Determinants of Antitrust Activity," *Journal of Law and Economics* 18, No. 2 (October 1975): 559-74.

11. Siegfried, p. 563.

12. Asch, Peter, "The Determinants and Effects of Antitrust Activity," *Journal of Law and Economics* 18, No. 2 (October 1975): 575-81.

13. Meehan, James W., and Michael H. Mann, "The Enforcement of Antitrust: Who Benefits?" Unpublished Working Paper #64, Boston College, 1974.

14. Bain, Joe S., *Industrial Organization*. New York: John Wiley and Sons, Inc., 1968.

15. Clabault, James M., and John F. Burton, *Sherman Act Indictments 1955-1965*. New York: Federal Legal Publications, 1966.

16. Meehan, p. 14.

17. Meehan, p. 17.

18. Meehan, p. 17.

19. Posner, 1970.

20. Stigler, George J., "The Economic Effect of the Antitrust Laws," *Journal of Law and Economics* 9 (October 1966): 225-38.

21. Stigler, p. 232.

22. Markham, Jesse W., "Mergers: The Adequacy of the New Section 7," in Almarin Phillips, editor, *Perspectives on Antitrust Policy*. Princeton: Princeton University Press, 1965, p. 166.

23. Markham, p. 175.

24. Mueller, Willard F., *The Celler-Kefauver Act: The First 27 Years,* a staff report to the Subcommittee on Monopolies and Commercial Law, 95th Congress, 2nd session, December 1978.

25. Mueller, p. 19.

26. Mueller, p. 70.

27. Elzinga, Kenneth G., "The Antimerger Law: Pyrrhic Victories?" *Journal of Law and Economics* 12, No. 1 (April 1969): 43-78.

28. Markham, p. 164.

29. Weiss, Leonard W., "An Analysis of the Allocation of Antitrust Division Resources," in James A. Dalton and Stanford L. Levin, editors, *The Antitrust Dilemma*. Lexington: D. C. Heath and Company, 1974.

30. Steiner, Peter O., *Mergers, Motives, Effects, Policies*. Ann Arbor: University of Michigan Press, 1975, p. 206.

31. Boyle, Stanley E., "Pre-merger Growth and Profit Characteristics of Large Conglomerate Mergers in the United States, 1948-1968," *Saint John's Law Review,* Special Edition (Spring 1970): 152-70.

32. Federal Trade Commission, *Economic Report on Conglomerate Merger Performance, An Empirical Analysis of Nine Corporations*. Washington, D.C.: U.S. Government Printing Office, 1972.

33. Reid, Samuel R., *Mergers, Managers, and the Economy*. New York: McGraw-Hill, 1968.

34. Hogarty, Thomas F., "'The Profitability of Corporate Mergers," *Journal of Business* 43, No. 3 (July 1970): 317-27.

35. Steiner, p. 206.

36. Steiner, p. 206.

37. Weston, J. Fred, *The Role of Mergers in the Growth of Large Firms*. Berkeley: University of California Press, 1953.

38. Nelson, Ralph L., *Merger Movements in American Industry 1895-1956*. National Bureau of Economic Research, General Studies No. 66. Princeton: Princeton University Press, 1959.

39. Nelson, p. 119.

40. Gort, Michael, "An Economic Disturbance Theory of Mergers." *Quarterly Journal of Economics* 83, No. 4 (November 1969): 624-42.

41. Leonard, William N., "Mergers, Industrial Concentration, and Antitrust Policy," *Journal of Economic Issues,* 10, No. 2 (June 1976): 354-81.

42. Beckenstein, Alan R., "Merger Activity and Merger Theories: An Empirical Investigation," *The Antitrust Bulletin,* 24, No. 1 (Spring 1979) 105-28.

Chapter 3

1. Weiss, Leonard W., "The Concentration-Profits Relationship and Antitrust," in Harvey J. Goldschmid, H. Michael Mann, and J. Fred Weston, editors, *Industrial Concentration: The New Learning*. Boston: Little, Brown and Company, 1974, p. 201.

2. Weiss, p. 202.

3. Collins, Norman R., and Lee E. Preston, "Price-Cost Margins and Industry Structure," *Review of Economics and Statistics,* (August 1969): 271-312.

4. Sassone, Peter G., and William Schaffer, *Cost-Benefit Analysis*. New York: Harcourt, Brace and Jovanovich, 1978.

5. Musgrave, Richard A., and Peggy B. Musgrave, *Public Finance in Theory and Practice*. New York: McGraw-Hill, 1973, p. 177.

6. Weiss, Leonard W., "An Analysis of the Allocation of Antitrust Resources," in James A. Dalton and Stanford L. Levin, editors, *The Antitrust Dilemma*. Lexington: D. C. Heath and Company, 1974.

7. Elzinga, Kenneth G., "The Antimerger Law: Pyrrhic Victories?" *Journal of Law and Economics* 12, No. 1 (April 1969): 43-78.

8. American Bar Association, Section of Antitrust Law, *Merger Case Digest*. Chicago: American Bar Association, 1972, p. 627.

9. Landes, William M., and Richard A. Posner, "Legal Precedent: a Theoretical and Empirical Analysis," *Journal of Law and Economics,* (Aug. 1976): 249-307.

10. *U.S. v. Trenton Potteries Co.,* 273 U.S. 392, 1927.

11. Landes, p. 263.

12. Mueller, Williard F., *The Celler-Kefauver Act: Sixteen Years of Enforcement,* a staff report to the Antitrust Subcommittee of the House Judiciary Committee, 90th Congress, 1st session, October 17, 1967.

13. *Brown Shoe v. U.S.,* 370 U.S. 294, 1962.

14. *U.S. v. Von's Grocery Co.,* 384 U.S. 270, 1966.

15. Stigler, George J., "The Economic Effect of the Antitrust Laws," *Journal of Law and Economics* 9 (October 1966): 225-38.

16. Harberger, Arnold C., "Monopoly and Resource Allocation," 44 *American Economic Review,* part 2, Paper and Proceedings (May 1954).

Chapter 4

1. Markham, Jesse W., "Mergers: The Adequacy of the New Section 7," in Almarin Phillips, editor *Perspectives on Antitrust Policy.* Princeton: Princeton University Press, 1965, p. 166.

2. Hausman, William J., "Comment: Mergers, Industrial Concentration, and Antitrust Policy," *Journal of Economic Issues,* 10, No. 2 (June 1976): 382-85.

3. Arnould, Richard J., "Comment: An Analysis of the Allocation of Antitrust Division Resources," in James A. Dalton and Stanford L. Levin, editors, *The Antitrust Dilemma.* Lexington: D. C. Heath and Company, 1974.

4. Nelson, Ralph L., *Merger Movements in American Industry, 1895-1956.* Princeton: Princeton University Press, 1959.

5. Eis, Carl, "The 1919-1930 Merger Movement in American Industry," Unpublished Ph.D. dissertation, C.U.N.Y., 1968.

6. Federal Trade Commission, *Stastitical Report on Mergers and Acquisitions.* Washington, D.C.: U.S. Government Printing Office, 1978, pp. 133-218.

7. Thorp, Willard L., "The Merger Movement," in *The Structure of Industry,* Temporary National Economic Committee, Monograph No. 27, 1941.

8. Federal Trade Commission, *Statistical Report: Value of Shipments Data by Product Class for the 1,000 Largest Manufacturing Companies of 1950.* Washington, D.C.: U.S. Government Printing Office, 1972.

9. Federal Trade Commission, *Statistical Report on Mergers and Acquisitions,* pp. 133-218.

10. Federal Trade Commission, 1972.

11. Maddala, G. S., *Econometrics.* New York: McGraw-Hill, 1977.

12. Mueller, Willard F., *The Celler-Kefauver Act: The First 27 Years,* a staff report to the Subcommittee on Monopolies and Commercial Law, 95th Congress, 2nd session, December, 1978.

13. American Bar Association, Section of Antitrust Law, *Merger Case Digest.* Chicago: American Bar Association, 1972.

14. U.S. Bureau of the Census, Department of Commerce, *Historical Statistics of the United States, Colonial Times to 1957.*

15. U.S. Bureau of the Census, Department of Commerce, *Historical Statistics of the United States, Colonial Times to 1957.*

16. Maddala, G. S., *Econometrics.* New York: McGraw-Hill, 1977.

Chapter 5

1. Mueller, Willard F., "Antitrust in a Planned Economy: An Anachronism or an Essential Complement?" *Journal of Economic Issues* 9, No. 2 (June 1975): 159-79.

2. U.S. Senate, 95th Congress, *Hearings Before the Subcommittee on Antitrust and Monopoly of the Committee on the Judiciary,* first session on Oversight of Antitrust Enforcement by the Federal Trade Commission and the Justice Department's Antitrust Division, Washington, D.C.: U.S. Government Printing Office, May 3, 4, 5, 11, and 12, 1977.

3. Audretsch, David B., United States General Accounting Office, Program and Analysis Division, "The Allocation of Antitrust Resources," Unpublished Working Paper, Summer 1978.

4. Long, William F., Richard Schramm and Robert Tollison, "The Economic Determinants of Antitrust Activity," *Journal of Law and Economics* 16, No. 2 (October 1973); 351-64.

5. Long, p. 358.

6. American Bar Association, Section of Antitrust Law, *Merger Case Digest.* Chicago: 1972.

7. *United States v. Bethlehem Steel Corp.,* 168 U.S. 576, 1958.

8. *United States v. Philadelphia National Bank,* 334 U.S. 363, 1963.

9. United States Department of Justice, *Antitrust Enforcement, The Antitrust Division: How it Works, Enforcement Plans,* Trade Regulation Reports, No. 326, Part II. Chicago: Commerce Clearing House, p. 4.

10. United States Department of Justice, Part II, p. 4.

11. United States Department of Justice, Part II, p. 19.

12. United States Department of Justice, Part II, pp. 20-21.

13. United States Department of Justice, Part II, p. 12.

14. United States Department of Justice, Part II, p. 19.

15. United States Senate, p. 459.

16. United States Department of Justice, *Antitrust Enforcement,* Trade Regulation Reports, No. 345, Part III. Chicago: Commerce Clearing House.

17. United States Department of Justice, Part III, p. 83.

18. Weiss, Leonard W., "An Analysis of the Allocation of Antitrust Division Resources," in James A. Dalton and Stanford L. Levin, editors, *The Antitrust Dilemma.* Lexington: D. C. Heath and Company, 1974, p. 44.

19. Mueller, Willard F., *The Celler-Kefauver Act: The First 27 Years,* a staff report to the Subcommittee on Monopolies and Commercial Law, 95th Congress, 2nd session, December, 1978, p. 119.

20. Weiss, p. 47.

Chapter 6

1. Preston, Lee E., and Norman R. Collins, "Price-Cost Margins and Industry Structure," *Review of Economics and Statistics* (Aug. 1969): 271-312.

2. Elzinga, Kenneth F., "The Antimerger Law: Pyrrhic Victories?" *Journal of Law and Economics* 12, No. 1 (April 1969): 43-78.

3. American Bar Association, Section of Antitrust Law, *Merger Case Digest.* Chicago: American Bar Association, 1972.

4. Mueller, Willard F., *The Celler-Kefauver Act: The First 27 Years,* a staff report to the Subcommittee on Monopolies and Commercial Law, 95th Congress, 2nd session, December 1978.

5. Federal Trade Commission, *Statistical Report: Value of Shipments Data by Product Class for the 1,000 Largest Manufacturing Companies of 1950.* Washington, D.C.: U.S. Government Printing Office, 1972.

6. *Merger Case Digest,* p. 82.

7. Elzinga, p. 48.

8. *Merger Case Digest,* p. 838.

9. Mueller, p. 169.

10. Weiss, Leonard W., "An Analysis of the Allocation of Antitrust Division Resources," in James A. Dalton and Stanford L. Levin, editors, *The Antitrust Dilemma.* Lexington. D. C. Heath and Company, 1974.

11. U.S. Bureau of the Census, Census of Manufacturers, 1972, *Special Report Series: Concentration Ratios In Manufacturing, MC 72* (SR)-2. Washington, D.C.: U.S. Government Printing Office, 1975.

12. *Merger Case Digest,* p. 490.

Bibliography

American Bar Association, Section of Antitrust Law, *Merger Case Digest.* Chicago: American Bar Association, 1972.

Arnould, Richard J., "Comment: An Analysis of the Allocation of Antitrust Division Resources," in James A. Dalton and Stanford L. Levin, editors, *The Antitrust Dilemma.* Lexington: D. C. Heath and Company, 1974.

Asch, Peter, "The Determinants and Effects of Antitrust Activity," *Journal of Law and Economics* 18, No. 2 (October 1975): 575-81.

Audretsch, David B., United States General Accounting Office, Program and Analysis Division, "The Allocation of Antitrust Resources," Unpublished Working Paper, Summer 1978.

Bain, Joe S., *Industrial Organization.* New York: John Wiley and Sons, Inc., 1968.

Beckenstein, Alan R., "Merger Activity and Merger Theories: An Empirical Investigation," *The Antitrust Bulletin,* 24, No. 1 (Spring 1979): 105-28.

Bork, Robert H., "Legislative Intent and the Policy of the Sherman Act," *Journal of Law and Economics* 60, (October 1966): 7-48.

Boyle, Stanley E., "Pre-merger Growth and Profit Characteristics of Large Conglomerate Mergers in the United States, 1948-1968," *Saint John's Law Review,* Special Edition (Spring 1970): 152-70.

Clabault, James M., and John F. Burton, *Sherman Act Indictments 1955-1965.* New York: Federal Legal Publications, 1966.

Collins, Norman R., and Lee E. Preston, "Price-Cost Margins and Industry Structure," *Review of Economics and Statistics,* (August 1969): 271-312.

Eis, Carl, "The 1919-1930 Merger Movement in American Industry," Unpublished Ph.D. dissertation, C.U.N.Y.: 1968.

_____, "The 1919-1930 Merger Movement in American Industry," *Journal of Law and Economics,* 12, No. 2 (October 1969): 267-96.

Elzinga, Kenneth G., "The Antimerger Law: Pyrrhic Victories?" *Journal of Law and Economics* 12, No. 1 (April 1969): 43-78.

Federal Trade Commission, *Economic Report on Conglomerate Merger Performance, An Empirical Analysis of Nine Corporations.* Washington, D.C.: U.S. Government Printing Office, 1972.

_____, *Statistical Report: Value of Shipments Data by Product Class for the 1,000 Largest Manufacturing Companies of 1950.* Washington, D.C.: U.S. Government Printing Office, 1972.

_____, *Statistical Report on Mergers and Acquisitions.* Washington, D.C.: U.S. Government Printing Office, 1978.

Galbraith, John K., *The New Industrial State*. Boston: Houghton Mifflin Company, 1967.

Gort, Michael, "An Economic Disturbance Theory of Mergers," *Quarterly Journal of Economics* 83, No. 4 (November 1969): 624-42.

Harberger, Arnold C., "Monopoly and Resource Allocation," 44 *American Economic Review,* part 2, Paper and Proceedings (May 1954).

Harbeson, Robert H., "The Clayton Act: Sleeping Giant of Antitrust?" *American Economic Review,* 1958.

Hausman, William J., "Comment: Mergers, Industrial Concentration, and Antitrust Policy," *Journal of Economic Issues,* 10, No. 2 (June 1976): 382-85.

Hogarty, Thomas F., "The Profitability of Corporate Mergers," *Journal of Business* 43, No. 3 (July 1970): 317-27.

Kamerschen, David R., "An Estimation of the 'Welfare Loss' from Monopoly in the American Economy," *Western Economic Journal* 4 (1966): 221-37.

Landes, William M., and Richard A. Posner, "Legal Precedent: a Theoretical and Empirical Analysis," *Journal of Law and Economics,* (August 1976): 249-307.

Leonard, William N., "Mergers, Industrial Concentration, and Antitrust Policy," *Journal of Economic Issues,* 10, No. 2 (June 1976): 354-81.

Long, William F., Richard Schramm and Robert Tollison, "The Economic Determinants of Antitrust Activity," *Journal of Law and Economics* 16, No. 2 (October 1973): 351-64.

Maddala, G. S., *Econometrics*. New York: McGraw-Hill, 1977.

Markham, Jesse W., "Mergers: The Adequacy of the New Section 7," in Almarin Phillips, editor, *Perspectives on Antitrust Policy,* Princeton: Princeton University Press, 1965.

Martin, David Dale, *Mergers and the Clayton Act*. Berkeley: University of California Press, 1959.

Meehan, James W., and Michael H. Mann, "The Enforcement of Antitrust: Who Benefits?" Unpublished Working Paper #64, Boston College, 1974.

Mueller, Willard F., "Antitrust in a Planned Economy: An Anachronism or an Essential Complement?" *Journal of Economic Issues* 9, No. 2 (June 1975): 159-79.

—————, *The Celler-Kefauver Act: Sixteen Years of Enforcement,* a staff report to the Antitrust Subcommittee of the House Judiciary Committee, 90th Congress, 1st session, October 17, 1967.

—————, *The Celler-Kefauver Act: The First 27 Years,* a staff report to the Subcommittee on Monopolies and Commercial Law, 95th Congress, 2nd session, December 1978.

Musgrave, Richard A., and Peggy B. Musgrave, *Public Finance in Theory and Practice*. New York: McGraw-Hill, 1973.

Nelson, Ralph L., *Merger Movements in American Industry 1895-1956*. National Bureau of Economic Research, General Studies No. 66. Princeton: Princeton University Presss, 1959.

Posner, Richard A., *Antitrust Law: An Economic Perspective*. Chicago: University of Chicago Press, 1976.

—————, "A Statistical Study of Antitrust Enforcement," *Journal of Law and Economics* 13, No. 2 (October 1970): 355-420.

—————, "The Federal Trade Commission," *University of Chicago Law Review* 52 (1969): 47-89.

Preston, Lee E. and Norman R. Collins, "Price-Cost Margins and Industry Structure," *Review of Economics and Statistics* (August 1969): 271-312.

Reid, Samuel R., *Mergers, Managers, and the Economy*. New York: McGraw-Hill, 1968.

Sassone, Peter G., and William Schaffer, *Cost-Benefit Analysis*. New York: Harcourt, Brace and Jovanovich, 1978.

Scherer, F. M., "The Posnerian Harvest: Separating Wheat from Chaff," *Yale Law Review* 86 (April 1977): 974-1002.

Schwartzman, David, "The Burden of Monopoly," *Journal of Political Economy* 68 (1960): 627-30.

Siegfried, John J., "The Determinants of Antitrust Activity," *Journal of Law and Economics* 18, No. 2 (October 1975): 559-74.

Steiner, Peter O., *Mergers, Motives, Effects, Policies*. Ann Arbor: University of Michigan Press, 1975.

Stigler, George J., "The Economic Effect of the Antitrust Laws," *Journal of Law and Economics* 9 (October 1966): 225-38.

──────, "Monopoly and Oligopoly by Merger," *American Economic Review Papers and Proceedings,* (May 1950).

Thorp, Willard L., "The Merger Movement," in *The Structure of Industry,* Temporary National Economic Committee, Monograph No. 27, 1941.

U.S. Bureau of the Census, Department of Commerce, *Historical Statistics of the United States, Colonial Times to 1957*. U.S. Government Printing Office, 1957.

──────, Census of Manufacturers, 1972, *Special Report Series: Concentration Ratios in Manufacturing, MC 72* (SR)-2. Washington, D.C.,: U.S. Government Printing Office, 1975.

United States Department of Justice, *Antitrust Enforcement, The Antitrust Division: How it Works, Enforcement Plans,* Trade Regulation Reports, No. 326, Part II. Chicago: Commerce Clearing House, p. 4.

──────, *Antitrust Enforcement,* Trade Regulation Reports, No. 345, Part III, Chicago: Commerce Clearing House.

U.S. Senate, 95th Congress, *Hearings Before the Subcommittee on Antitrust and Monopoly of the Committee on the Judiciary,* first session on Oversight of Antitrust Enforcement by the Federal Trade Commission and the Justice Department's Antitrust Division, Washington, D.C.: U.S. Government Printing Office, May 3, 4, 5, 11, and 12, 1977.

Weiss, Leonard W., "An Analysis of the Allocation of Antitrust Division Resources," in James A. Dalton and Stanford L. Levin, editors, *The Antitrust Dilemma*. Lexington: D. C. Heath and Company, 1974.

──────, "The Concentration-Profits Relationship and Antitrust," in Harvey J. Goldschmid, H. Michael Mann, and J. Fred Weston, editors, *Industrial Concentration: The New Learning*. Boston: Little, Brown and Company, 1974.

Weston, J. Fred, *The Role of Mergers in the Growth of Large Firms*. Berkeley: University of California Press, 1953.

Index